The Science of Homeschooling

Empowering Parents to Manage Their Children's Education

By Kristy Crandall

The Science of Homeschooling

Empowering Parents to Manage their Children's Education

By Kristy Crandall

A special thank you to the parents whose questions inspired this book.
Thank you to the parents who shared their stories, and to those who love their children fiercely- who are brave enough to do what they believe is best for their children, even if it is not the most common.
Thank you for not accepting the way things are as the only way they can be, but for having the courage to be a trailblazer, and for teaching your children to do the same.
Thank you for being involved and intentional regarding your children's education. Their future, and society, will be better because of it.

Table of Contents

An Introduction to Homeschooling

Homeschooling has been a somewhat ambiguous idea for most people in the recent past. There have been a lot of narratives pushed about the homeschool lifestyle with varying levels of credibility. Some are good, some are bad; many tend to be more of the exception than the rule. Nevertheless, the stories that have been spun lead to some confusion among outsiders as to the true nature of homeschooling. This book is an attempt to remedy that, and to encourage parents that, though daunting, homeschooling is a possible, worthwhile venture that often leads to better parent-child relationships and more well-rounded individuals.

Homeschooling, quite simply, is teaching children academic principles, religion, and life skills at home. In the early years, the academic portion often includes math, writing, and reading, along with some basic science, and maybe some art or music studies. In upper elementary school it may also include foreign language, history, grammar, logic, social studies; and high school may also include government, rhetoric, debate, home economics, financial planning, and a variety of interest-specific hobbies and classes. Core classes are often influenced by the requirements of the state (Homeschool Legal Defense Association, 2021), but additional classes are selected based on personal interest and the values of the individual family.

There are a variety of different approaches and curricula that parents choose to utilize with their children, but the hallmark of homeschooling is flexibility. Parents have the freedom to choose their approach to teaching, as well as their timetable for doing it; some parents adhere to the traditional nine-month school year with breaks according to the local public-school schedule, while others opt to do school year-round, three days a week, or with customized breaks for family trips or major family events, such as new babies, moves, or family emergencies.

Parents also have the flexibility to speed up or slow down at various points in accordance with their students' abilities and weaknesses. Sometimes, children pick up on a concept very quickly and can move on; other times, they struggle, and even need to take a break and revisit the concept at a later time. Rather than repeating a concept ad nauseum, homeschool parents have the ability to step away from it for a while, and return to it at a later date when a child is better prepared and less frustrated.

In addition, homeschool parents have the ability to change their approach if a student doesn't seem to be grasping a concept well. This can mean supplementing with something different, or even switching to a new curriculum in the middle of the year to suit their needs. Unlike public school, where teachers are often limited in their time and resources and forced to resort to a checking-the-boxes and memorizing-the-answers approach to learning, so that students often graduate with only a rudimentary understanding of critical concepts, such as reading, writing, and math (Allen, 2016), homeschool families have the luxury of being able to alter their approach so a concept is easier to comprehend. This individualized approach helps to ensure that students intimately learn the information for themselves, instead of "slipping through the cracks" of an over-extended, one-size-fits-all methodology.

Homeschooling often focuses on quality, not quantity. A typical homeschool day is often only 2-3 hours of focused work for lower levels, and 4-5 hours for high school. This means that children have more time to explore their own interests, participate in extracurricular activities, and get more sleep. Homeschoolers do not usually have homework assignments to do, because they get all of their schoolwork done during the course of the day. This shorter, more focused, and flexible approach makes it easier for children to give their attention to their studies.

One of the most advantageous elements of homeschooling is the ability for real-world learning. Homeschool students are often involved in day-to-day household activities, as well as their studies. This means that they are educated, not only in skills necessary for employment, but also keenly aware of the responsibilities of running a home. During a school day, a student may accompany their parent to the bank and discuss the reason for the visit; they may go to the grocery store and calculate the price per ounce of a specific item; they may take an impromptu field trip to an excavation site or to the zoo.

Homeschooling is less of a "thing to do" and more of a lifestyle for many families. It is about gently coaching students to be equipped to live confidently and competitively in the "real world" once they leave home. This includes unstructured social interactions with people of all ages and backgrounds, exposure to a variety of environments, and participation in numerous activities to challenge and stretch the child and help them discover their talents and interests.

It is difficult to accurately describe something that is as amorphous as homeschooling. The truth is, it is as unique for each family as the family itself. Let this be an encouragement as you begin to explore the possibilities of homeschooling together. There isn't a right or wrong way to do it.

Homeschooling is very much a journey- of learning what works for your family and what doesn't; becoming intimately acquainted with your children's learning styles and your own approach to teaching. It's a quest for the happy medium where the children learn, trust is built, and frustration is kept to a minimum. That is probably the hardest thing to wrap one's mind around as a new homeschooler- kids just need to learn the basics; and, if they still love learning when that's done, and are equipped and motivated to learn things on their own, that's a true homeschool success story!

The Academic Case for Homeschooling

"…Last, but not least, every child wants to know. There they are, those desires, ready to act on occasion and our business is to make due use of this natural provision for the work of education. We do make use of the desires, not wisely, but too well. We run our schools upon emulation, the desire of every child to be first; and not the ablest, but the most pushing, comes to the front. We quicken emulation by the common desire to get and to have, that is, by the impulse of avarice. So we offer prizes, exhibitions, scholarships, every incentive that can be proposed. We cause him to work for our approbation, we play upon his vanity, and the boy does more than he can. What is the harm, we say, when all those springs of action are in the child already? The athlete is beginning to discover that he suffers elsewhere from the undue development of any set of muscles; and the boy whose ambition, or emulation, has been unduly stimulated becomes a flaccid person. But there is a worse evil. We all want knowledge just as much as we want bread. We know it is possible to cure the latter appetite by giving more stimulating food; and the worst of using other spurs to learning is that a natural love of knowledge which should carry us through eager school-days, and give a spice of adventure to the duller days of mature life, is effectually choked; and boys and girls 'cram to pass but not to know; they do pass but they don't know.' The divine curiosity which should have been an equipment for life hardly survives early schooldays." (Mason, 2017)

Charlotte Mason was a teacher in England in the early 1900s. Although she taught thousands of children, in her later years she began teaching parents and caregivers on how children learn and thrive best. She stressed the importance of giving children exposure to a wide variety of ideas and experiences, and giving them the freedom to interpret the information for themselves. She believed in encouraging curiosity, and guiding self-motivated learning for the sake of understanding, rather than force-feeding information that was disconnected from the world the children lived in. She believed that all children had the capacity to learn in this way- in a society where poor children learned a trade rather than receiving a formal education- regardless of their social or economic "advantage," because all children are born with the capacity to observe and create their own ideas accordingly.

To varying degrees, homeschool families largely subscribe to this same philosophy in the instruction of their children. While textbooks and worksheets are often used, there is a more pronounced focus on real-world, experiential learning, which is more engaging and increases retention; textbook concepts are often reinforced through practical application, so there is a better understanding of their relevance for real life. This may contribute to the results of a recent study by the National Home Education Research Institute, which concluded, "The home-educated typically score 15 to 30 percentile points above public-school students on standardized academic achievement tests" (Brian D. Ray, 2021). These percentages were even more pronounced in minority students. In addition, "Research facts on homeschooling show that the home-educated are doing well, typically above average, on measures of social, emotional, and psychological development. Research measures include peer interaction, self-concept, leadership skills, family cohesion, participation in community service, and self-esteem" (Brian D. Ray, 2021).

The academic advantage of homeschooling extends beyond the elementary and secondary education years. Alpha Omega Publications states, "The high achievement level of homeschoolers is readily recognized by recruiters from some of the best colleges in the nation…Schools such as Massachusetts Institute of Technology, Harvard, Stanford, and Duke University all actively recruit homeschoolers" (Why Colleges are Recruiting Homeschoolers, 2013).

"Educational consultant and former homeschool mom Dori Staehle recruited both homeschool and public school students in her job as a college admissions counselor. Staehle said that schools have caught on to the fact that homeschoolers represent a desirable pool of talent, often possessing impressive reading lists, letters of recommendation, AP credits, and experience in volunteering and the arts" (Why Colleges are Recruiting Homeschoolers, 2013).

Business Insider states, "…the term "homeschooling" is actually kind of a misnomer: Learning at home is only part of the equation. It's really about involving the surrounding community in raising the kids — that's when education starts to excel. Away from the standardized tests and rigid schedules in public education, kids can let their creative sides flourish, learn about the world they live in, and, when it's time, earn acceptance into the best colleges in the world" (Weller, 2015).

While homeschooled students thrive academically, in the early years and through college, public school students tend to struggle. "According to research…just under 40 percent of students score at college and career ready levels on NAEP. "College and career ready" means these scores strongly predict that students will be able to succeed doing college-level academics, or with on-the-job training in a position requiring only a high school diploma" (Kamenetz, 2016). This contrast is shocking, especially when one considers that taxpayers pay an average of $15,000 per year, per public school student (Brian D. Ray, 2021).

It is daunting to undertake a task as monumental as homeschooling, and to know that your children rely on you to prepare them for the "real world" later. However, there is a lot of evidence to support the positive outcome for students taught at home, regardless of the education level of their parents (Brian D. Ray, 2021). Homeschool parents are able to give their children unparalleled attention and a much more personalized education experience than even the best overworked teacher. Children learn the most through experiences, and experiences are much easier to have with the flexibility of a homeschool environment.

Brain Development in Early Childhood

Special attention is given to young children's development in this chapter, because early childhood is often overlooked as a time of learning; however, it is vitally important, as it sets the stage for the rest of their lives. In the early years, brain development occurs primarily through sensory experiences and tactile play. Allowing children time and resources to explore the world around them and develop their fine motor skills early increases their confidence in manipulating their environments, but it also sets them up for success academically- in kindergarten and beyond.

"Scientists now believe that to achieve the precision of the mature brain, stimulation in the form of movement and sensory experiences during the early developing years is necessary. Experience appears to exert its effects by strengthening and bonding synapses, which are the connections that are made between neurons. Connections that are not made by activity, or are weak, are "pruned away," much like the pruning of dead or weak branches of a tree. If the neurons are used, they become integrated into the circuitry of the brain. Due to differences in experience, not even identical twins are wired the same" (Carl Gabbard, 2015)

Many parents, in an attempt to give their children a jumpstart academically, opt to begin a sort of formal education before traditional school begins. Though well-intentioned, their children's young brains are not yet equipped for that form of learning, and it can lead to frustration and focus issues. Many studies suggest that a later start to the formal education process can actually be more advantageous in the long run, and in Finland- one of the most academically successful countries in the world- this is common practice.

"Central to early years education in Finland is a "late" start to schooling. At Franzenia, as in all Finnish daycare centres, the emphasis is not on maths, reading or writing (children receive no formal instruction in these until they are seven and in primary school) but creative play...

Daycare is to help them develop good social habits: to learn how to make friends and respect others, for example, or to dress themselves competently. Official guidance also emphasises the importance in pre-school of the "joy of learning", language enrichment and communication. There is an emphasis on physical activity (at least 90 minutes outdoor play a day). "Kindergarten in Finland doesn't focus on preparing children for school academically," writes the Finnish educational expert Pasi Sahlberg. "Instead the main goal is to make sure that the children are happy and responsible individuals"' (Butler, No GrammarSchools, Lots of Play: the Secrets of Europe's Top EducationSystem, 2016).

In 2016, Psychology Today reported on a study conducted by the National Institute of Child Health and Human Development, which observed young children for a period of time- some cared for at home, and others sent to daycare for varying lengths of time. Their conclusion was: "The type and quality of care can influence many aspects of development—including memory, language development, school readiness, math and reading achievement, the nature of relationships with parents and teachers, social skills, work habits, and behavioral adjustment—at least through grade school" (Marano, 2007). While there were a couple of benefits to daycare, such as better short-term memory and cognitive (academic) development, they also identified a number of issues, as well, including: increased behavioral problems and conflict with parents and teachers, an inability to work independently or utilize good time-management skills in grade school, and a negative impact on children's ability to problem solve and resolve conflict with peers.

These are just a few examples that illustrate the importance of play and unstructured time for exploration and experimentation for the healthy development of a young child. It also suggests that parental involvement is more important than people often acknowledge.

In a society that enthusiastically utilizes electronics and daycare centers as a means of monitoring and pacifying them, children are struggling increasingly with fine motor skills, focus and interpersonal relationships. Do children who spend their time weaving twigs and climbing on rocks have as much need for occupational therapy as those who grow up primarily in structured, sedentary environments? Do children with more varied, positive social interactions grow up to be more empathetic and respectful? It is worth investigating.

There is a lot of emphasis placed on academic performance worldwide. While it is important, it is not the only rubric for success. In fact, it is a very small part of what constitutes success. Academics can be learned at virtually any point in a person's life; it is not uncommon to see middle aged, or even more mature individuals returning to school to complete high school, college, or other continuing education. However, children who miss out on play and positive interactions while their brains are growing are shown to struggle more academically, socially, and mentally in their later years. There is very little that can be done to further develop a brain that has already passed that phase of growth.

It is also important to note that toddlers and young children are imitators- they learn by doing what they see others doing, even if the people they are watching are on television (Shrier, 2014). So, it is especially important to be mindful of the influences affecting one's children.

Homeschool children have the advantage of more encounters with older children and adults, rather than children their age- who are also lacking maturity and self-control. Since young children are imitators, it is very advantageous to surround them with positive influences- people who act out the traits one wants them to learn. This gives them a unique understanding and preparedness for life outside of the daycare center or classroom, so they are equipped to interact and do business with others more naturally and from an earlier age.

This is not meant to be a critique of any person or lifestyle. Rather, this is a challenge that we need to take a good, hard look at the way things are done, and whether it could be done better. Just because things are the way they are, and have been that way for a while, doesn't mean they cannot- or should not- be changed;

especially since time and research have shown that the current

education system leaves a lot to be desired

Building a Relationship of Trust

From the very beginning, children rely on the people around them to help them navigate the world they are born into. They learn from experience, interaction, trial and error, observation, and discussion. Their value in the world is largely influenced by the perceived judgements of the people around them.

In the early years, physical touch and sensory activities are especially important. According to a study published by Pediatrics and Child Health: "Developmental delay is often seen in children receiving inadequate or inappropriate sensory stimulation. For example, orphaned infants exposed to the bleakest of conditions in eastern European institutions exhibited impaired growth and cognitive development, as well as an elevated incidence of serious infections and attachment disorders" (Evan L Ardiel, 2010). This is an extreme example that highlights the importance of positive, personal investment in the life of a child.

As a child ages and begins to ask questions, communication becomes increasingly more important, and time and consideration for the incessant "whys" is crucial as they delve into something more than a surface-level understanding of the world. These relationships continue to be important as the child matures and grows through adolescence, into adulthood, and beyond. Children learn quickly, who will be there to help them make sense of the chaos in the world.

In the busyness of life, it is easy to overlook the significance of interactions with these little people who are eagerly trying to fit into the world around them. It is easy to become impatient and frustrated, and even to feel inadequate- like they require more time and attention than one can reasonably give. The idea of passing off the responsibility to someone else can seem appealing.

The purpose of this section is simply to emphasize that the interactions that one has with their children are important. And, if circumstances dictate that one must leave their children in the care of someone else, one must be especially diligent, because those interactions create impressions, and those impressions have an impact on who one's children will become. Parents must act as gatekeepers when it comes to the people and situations their children are exposed to. The interactions that people have with children, and the parents' compliance with negative situations ultimately make or break trust.

One of the big advantages to homeschooling, is that it is much easier to act as "gatekeeper" to the people and content that children are exposed to. This, by no means, suggests that homeschoolers are isolated; rather, parents carefully select positive interactions for their children throughout the week. This may include play dates with other homeschoolers, field trips to various attractions throughout the city (many zoos and children's museums host special events for homeschoolers during the week), music lessons, art classes, cooperative classes with other families, errands, and so on. Whatever the choices may be, they are selected to be enriching to the child's life and educational experience; and, families are able to experience them together. These positive experiences promote confidence and independence in children, and also help to develop trust and positive memories between parent and child.

In contrast, consider the amount of time that children spend in school if they are participating in public education. If a child is attending school for eight hours a day, they may only be home for about five hours in the evening before bedtime. If the child eats dinner and has two hours of homework per night, that means there may only be an hour or two left to spend together as a family in the evening, when everyone is tired. Families may have weekends together, but comparatively that is a much smaller amount of time.

A person is going to live life and build trust with those who are present and engaged during big life events. If a child spends most of their time surrounded by peers- good influences and bad- they are the ones they will develop the closest relationships with. A parent may not even be aware of the child's true personality or aspirations if they spend so much time apart, much less the influences that their child is being exposed to day to day.

Every quality relationship requires time and effort, and that means being present and accessible to answer questions and coach them through the sticky spots. For most homeschool families, the ability to truly get to know each other and experience things together is a big part of the homeschooling decision, as well as the ability to better manage the influences on impressionable minds. A parent who is present and aware of unpredicted situations that come up is better able to address them in the moment or initiate a conversation about them later on.

The ability to help a young mind navigate new and uncertain experiences is a privilege to be treasured, and it is a powerful tool for building trust to last a lifetime. As children grow through all of the different stages of life, one of the best gifts a parent can give them is an anchor- a place of certainty that they know they can return to and be loved unconditionally; a place they can always call home.

Find Your Village

As was stated earlier, homeschooling is very much about surrounding a child with a variety of positive experiences. It is not about being an expert on everything, so much as it is about finding people who are more knowledgeable to teach one's children about the subjects they are trying to learn. This not only means that they receive much better quality of education on a wider variety of subjects, but it also further develops their socialization and adaptation skills as their environment and interactions are constantly changing. This is why homeschoolers are often very comfortable talking to people of all ages, not just those who are their own age.

To familiarize their children with more of a classroom setting, many homeschool families choose to get involved in a local homeschool co-op. Homeschool co-ops consist of multiple families meeting together at set intervals to play, socialize, and learn. Parents teach classes according to their skills or interests, and all students in the age group are able to participate. These kinds of classes are helpful for teaching subjects such as public speaking, debate, drama, and others that are better suited to a group environment. Co-ops are also able to get group discounts for field trips at many locations throughout the city. Classes are often held at churches or community centers.

Homeschool co-ops are beneficial for parents, too, because it is a good place to connect with others who have similar experiences and struggles, so parents can share notes and help each other if they get stuck. New homeschoolers can connect with parents who are more experienced, and veteran homeschool parents are usually more than happy to share their wisdom with others.

Homeschool families look out for each other. There is a special bond that families share, simply for making the education of their children a priority. Not only do they share ideas, but they may also help each other with childcare, share books, clothes, and other resources amongst themselves to help cut costs where possible.

Besides co-ops, there are a number of other ways for homeschoolers to get involved in the community. Many cities have homeschool sports teams, drama groups, robotics and special interest clubs, and more! There are also special science days at many children's museums, demonstrations at zoos, and even small carpentry project days at hardware stores. Older students may take college classes, have jobs, participate in politics, or take a more active role in their community- many such endeavors become relevant on college admissions forms, and can help significantly to set the student apart from their peers.

Groups of homeschoolers are often able to get discounts for other field trips they choose to take, as well; and, because they do all of these things while most people are at work or school, these various exhibits and outings often have very few people visiting during these times. The HSLDA website also has a search feature, to connect families with support groups in their area. It can be found here: https://my.hslda.org/groups/s/.

Homeschool parents will be the first to say that no one person can do it on their own. Life happens, and it becomes hard at times to stay completely engaged in everything that is required to be the primary caregiver and educator of one's children. Homeschoolers readily admit that no one person does all things well or is qualified to teach all courses; however, that is what makes the "village mentality" so important. Homeschooling is less about knowing and being all of the things all of the time, and more about seeking out people whose strengths are contrary to one's own, so children have opportunities to experience things and grow in ways that would be difficult to do with just one teacher.

Homeschooling is about surrounding oneself with other people who value children and have a passion to help them grow into the best versions of themselves. They do this by investing in each other's children, and by providing opportunities for the children to engage together in a variety of structured and unstructured environments.

Children who grow up in this sort of environment thrive. They learn to be confident interacting with people of all ages, to be self-motivated, to adapt, to communicate and network, to manage time well, and they have a variety of different experiences and knowledge of an assortment of different topics.

Ultimately, homeschooling is about being resourceful, flexible, and creative. Many people find themselves in situations where they do not have a good support system in place. In these situations, one must work with what they have and make the most of it. Many farms and small businesses are happy to let homeschoolers tour their establishment; and many senior citizens, or those who no longer have children at home, would love the opportunity to be involved in the lives of young ones again. If there are physical limitations that make leaving home difficult, many places now offer virtual tours, or there are websites, such as www.outschool.com, that offer online courses that are in many peoples' budgets.

Having a good support system in place is very helpful while homeschooling, as it is during most other periods of life, but a child can still learn and thrive in a home environment if that is not available to them. The people that children most need invested in their lives are their parents or caretakers.

Real-World, Experiential Learning

"The history of education shows that up to 50 years ago, education was principally geared towards getting a job. That's no longer the case, it seems. If we could agree on the purpose of education…, then we can agree the curriculum to fulfill that purpose. Everything else follows. And there may be more than one purpose and there may be more than one curriculum. One size doesn't fit all" (Schoolsmith, 2019).

Children should know more than how to fill in bubble answers when they leave school. They should be confident in their abilities to think and to reason, and be able to adapt to whatever environment they're put into. They should be able to speak with respect and a deeply held belief that they have something valuable to say. Children should be able to step into the real world and say,

"I've seen this before, and I know what to do; this time, I'm just doing it on my own."

That is a hard goal to attain when children spend forty or more hours a week sitting in a classroom, surrounded by the same people and the same predictable environment. In a survey of 165,000 high school students, "An overwhelming number of students, 87 percent, want to eventually earn a college degree and land a career. But many believe that their schools aren't helping them develop the skills they'll need to succeed after graduation" (Leal, 2015).

In the grand scheme of things, "school age" represents a very small part of peoples' lives. It is also the period in which their brains are developing and growing to survive in the world they are living in. It does not make sense for them to spend a significant amount of time in a classroom setting for thirteen to twenty years, in a stagnant and predictable environment, only to be thrown out into the chaos of a world that demands improvisation and a plethora of skills that are never taught in school. Is it any wonder that they feel lost when they are suddenly expected to integrate into the world as good and productive citizens? Students who are forced to drop out to help take care of their families understand, better than most, that there is a disconnect between what most schools offer and what they need to succeed, or even just to survive, in their real-life situations.

Academic learning is important, but it needs to have evident real-life applications. Children- especially young children- thrive when they are able to learn things that are "real" and relevant. They love to help out with what they see adults doing, because that's how they learn to become a part of the same world.

"Learning is the holistic process of adaptation. Learning is not just the result of cognition, but involves the integrated functioning of the total person- thinking, feeling, perceiving, and behaving. It encompasses other specialized models of adaptation from the scientific method to problem solving, decision making, and creativity" (Angela Passarelli, 2011).

Teaching children is much like planting a garden. If you are planting a garden, most people know that it is not enough to simply scatter seeds and water them incessantly. Plants need much more than just water. They grow best if they are planted at the proper time of year; they need room to grow; and proper soil that is well-drained, nutrient rich, and the proper pH. Plants need the proper amount of sunlight, good air flow, protection from extreme elements, and they need time.

However, planting a garden is more complicated than that. Because different plants have different individual needs; some plants grow well next to each other, and others inhibit each other's growth. So, it's beneficial to strategically plant to allow for optimal growth.

Even if all of these considerations are accounted for with complete precision, plants will grow at different rates. Even multiple plants of the same variety will not grow exactly the same. But, eventually, if their needs are met, all plants should grow strong and hearty- the best version of themselves they can be.

In contrast, if seeds are scattered without much forethought or prep work, they will not grow as well. If the new seedlings are watered incessantly to get them to grow, some will grow, but many will drown. It is easy for the plants to become waterlogged, and many will rot or become diseased. Without good sunlight, plants will become "leggy"- tall and weak; without good airflow they will develop mildew or other fungus; without balanced nutrients, leaves will yellow or growth will be stunted- some will do ok, but most will struggle to grow, and almost none will reach their full potential. Water is essential for growth, but too much water, or not enough of other essentials, makes it almost impossible for plants to grow well.

In the same way, academics are important. But, focusing exclusively on academics for the first thirteen, or more, years of life means that children's development becomes very lopsided, and they are ill-equipped to "withstand the elements" when they arise. It used to be, that academics were secondary to the needs of the family and learning the family trade. For many years, school was a luxury that only the wealthiest families were able to provide for their children.

It is a huge blessing that virtually every child now is able to be educated; however, we seem to have reached the other end of the pendulum, where children are well-versed in the things they are taught in school, but they don't have practical experience or knowledge of much else. Instead of having a family trade to fall back on, children now are stuck living at home, because they go through school and then feel ill-equipped to do anything once their school tenure is done.

School was never intended to replace home learning, but was meant to be an addition to it, to enhance individuals' abilities to thrive and provide for their families. Reading, writing, and math make it possible for people to gain knowledge independently, communicate ideas, and engage in fair business transactions. These skills are essential for success in business and in life. But, on their own they leave much to be desired, because there is no context in which to use them.

Until there is practical application for even these basic skills, they are just abstract ideas that possess very little real-world significance. Perhaps that is what is missing most from the modern approach to education- people used to understand the need for these basic skills so there was a desire to learn them. Today, many people seem to have lost sight of the context and practical application for these skills, so there is very little perceived value in knowing how to do them. Children who are more involved in real-world activities better understand the importance of these skills and have a greater appreciation for school.

Room to Breathe

"Children learn in their own time and style. A teacher in a classroom of ten students could not expect all ten to learn in the same way. Some students will learn best visually through looking and observing. Other students will learn best from listening to their parents, their peers and the sounds and noises that fill their environment. There are also students that will learn best from a "hands-on" approach and need to touch, feel and "do" in order to learn best" (Allison Metsch, 2019).

One of the most appealing aspects of homeschooling is the flexibility it affords to students. Every student is as unique in their learning style as they are in their personality, so it is simply unrealistic to expect a teacher in a classroom of thirty students to be able to teach each student in the way they learn best. Even the most devoted teacher will fail in this impossible task. It makes much more sense for a parent, who should already know their child better than anyone, to facilitate learning for each of their children in a way that is best suited to the individual child.

When a child is able to learn in the way best suited to them, it makes the learning process infinitely easier and more enjoyable. Additionally, and perhaps more importantly, ease of learning promotes self-confidence in the student, and thereby sets them up for greater future success.

According to researchers Bruce W. Tuckman and Thomas L. Sexton, "comparisons between self-believers, the self-unsure, and self-doubters showed that self-believers perform the most, outperform even their own self-expectations, and are unaffected by most external conditions while self-doubters perform the least (almost nothing), underperform even their own self-expectations, but perform more in structured, well-defined situations with the opportunity for goal-setting and planning beforehand and feedback afterward" (Bruce W. Tuckman, 1992).

Teaching the student in a way that makes sense to them helps to promote better self-confidence, which, in turn, improves performance. Self-confidence also influences students to be more self-motivated- to work on their own and to explore new ideas.

"At the National Institute of Education in Singapore, professors Lazar Stankov, Suzanne Morony, and Lee Yim Ping have found that students who think they are skilled in math tend to perform well on math tests... 'From this study, we know that confidence is a much better predictor of students' achievements than any other non-cognitive measure,' notes Lazar. 'In fact, it acts in a way that it overcomes everything else; so confidence is very important'" (Briggs, 2014).

Dr. Nate Zinsser describes it this way: "...human confidence is very much a psychological "bank account," a repository of your thoughts about yourself and what is happening in your life. Just as the balance of any bank account at the end of the day depends upon how much is either deposited into it or withdrawn from it, the psychological bank account of confidence also rises and falls depending on how you are thinking at any moment. "Deposit" into that bank account memories of past successes, memories of progress or improvement, and thoughts about future improvements and accomplishments, and the "balance" grows. "Withdraw" from that account by replaying past setbacks and difficulties, or by fixating on possible future setbacks and difficulties, and the "balance" shrinks" (Zinsser, 2022).

Dr. Zinsser illustrates the importance of facilitating good memories for the "psychological bank account" of impressionable students. This is most easily done by providing opportunities, whenever possible, for them to learn through their strengths rather than forcing them to struggle through their weaknesses. This is virtually impossible to do in a classroom setting, but is relatively easy to accomplish at home.

Flexibility in education doesn't just mean the freedom to cater to an individual's learning style, but also the ability to modify one's learning schedule. Whether a student is overwhelmed by an idea and needs to take a break for a while, or there is a family emergency that requires one's attention, homeschoolers have the ability to move things around, or stop completely for a time, so that the education process is less intimidating.

Some families forego the nine month, five days a week learning schedule that schools adhere to, and instead they opt to do school three days a week throughout the year. Families may also schedule school years around major life events, such as new babies, moves, family trips, etc. Homeschooling means there is flexibility to take breaks when needed or move schoolwork around to accommodate life, without missing out on any of the important lessons they would while in school.

Many military families find home education to be much less stressful, because they can coordinate their school years around moves and avoid the hassle of starting at a new school mid-year. There is much more freedom to coordinate around life events and family emergencies, which is how formal education used to be.

Homeschool families are also able to modify some elements of their curriculum to explore personal interests- especially in regard to science, history, art, music, and other more elective classes. A student who expresses an interest in a subject that isn't specifically in the plan for the current year, may still be able to include it into their schoolwork for whatever length of time the parent deems appropriate.

Flexibility in homeschooling looks like different things in different families, but the goal is the same- to integrate education into life, instead of life into education, and to make the learning process as organic, easy, and enjoyable as possible. Learning that happens organically tends to be remembered better, and it fosters greater and greater curiosity.

Well-Fed Curiosity

"…a "hungry mind" is a core determinant of individual differences in academic achievement" (Sophie von Stumm, 2011). This has been the conclusion of numerous studies in recent times, as people seek to understand the learning process and how to increase its effectiveness; it is not enough simply to present the information to a child and expect them to absorb it, but studies suggest that an interest in the subject increases retention of material, and even activates the reward centers of the brain, so individuals receive satisfaction from learning (Min Jeong Kang, 2009).

What this means, is when a person learns about something they are interested in, it releases chemicals in the brain that make the individual feel happy, similar to eating chocolate, doing drugs, etc. This also suggests that, for the curious mind, learning has a somewhat addictive effect; the good feeling associated with learning incentivizes them to keep trying to learn. Active engagement of this nature improves retention of the information learned.

"Curiosity is thought to be enhanced when individuals are allowed to engage in activities that are personally meaningful. As such, it is believed that interventions which promote an experience of meaningfulness of an activity might enhance a child's engagement in that activity, and help foster curiosity" (Prachi E. Shah, 2018).

Many teachers do go to great lengths to try and make their subject matter interesting. They may use colorful graphics, informational videos, activities, field trips, guest speakers, and other aids to help make learning more exciting for their students. However, from a practical standpoint, even the most phenomenal teachers are limited in what they can provide for their most inquisitive students.

Public school teachers are limited by time and curriculum parameters. There is little room to deviate from the agreed upon lessons, and it would be impossible to satisfy the curiosities of every student in the class without foregoing some of the pre-planned lessons.

A pediatric research journal on the subject states: "Currently, most classroom interventions have focused on the cultivation of early effortful control and a child's self-regulatory capacities, but our results suggest that an alternate message, focused on the importance of curiosity, should also be considered" (Prachi E. Shah, 2018). This latter approach- which seeks to foster the natural curiosity in a child- is found much more frequently in homeschool environments. Though they often follow a curriculum, homeschool days are usually shorter, so there is more time to explore personal interests and dally in imaginative play. Since homeschooling typically means fewer children to tend to, it is easier to take "detours" in the education process as special opportunities come about, or as curiosity beckons.

For example, a family may decide one day to take a trip to a local museum. While there, their oldest son notices an exhibit about airplanes and aerodynamics. He may go home excited and intrigued by what he has just seen, and ask to explore it further, instead of the scheduled lesson on the solar system. The solar system lesson can wait for another day, and his parent may choose to allow him a day or a week to explore aerodynamics on his own. They may go to the library to find books on the subject, or look online for interesting videos or documentaries- maybe they will even examine the similarities and differences between the wings of airplanes and the wings of birds. An older boy may also delve into the physics involved in flight and determining how well something will fly.

Maybe from there, he will stumble upon a book about catapults and decide he wants to try to build one. He may find a blueprint and assemble one on his own, and experiment with adjusting the length of the arm, or changing the payload. This may expand into a lesson on geometry, and determining where an item

will land based on where it was released.

Maybe this boy will decide he wants to be a physics major;

or, maybe he will simply have a better understanding of the world

and the laws that govern it. The point is, that he has some control

over the direction of his learning, and as a result he will likely

learn things that he never would have otherwise. And, he will

remember them; because it is something that he was curious about,

and he followed that curiosity through various twists and turns, and

engaged with the material at a greater depth than he would have in

a classroom.

Allowing children the freedom to explore their interests

unhindered provides a unique window into their personalities and

passions. It may help them find their desired career path at a young

age.

While the curriculum may need to be completed eventually,

allowing children the freedom to explore their curiosities

oftentimes fosters more curiosity and an independent work ethic that extends beyond just the original topic that caught their interest. Children who are curious tend to search out other topics to take an interest in, so they can experience that "reward" when they find what they are looking for. The give and take that is possible with homeschooling makes the learning process much less tedious for everyone, and it helps to develop positive habits that will be invaluable in later years.

The Self-Motivated Student

Parents and teachers alike dream of self-motivated students. Unfortunately for most, it is only a dream. Most students hate school, and educators have come to expect that the road to literate pupils will be an uphill battle full of sweat, tears, and some who will not make it.

There is a lot of debate and speculation surrounding the factors that actually cause a child to fail or to succeed; many of them are beyond their educator's control- intelligence, personality, demographic, home life- they are important factors that teachers must accept and embrace as they strive to teach their charges all that they are supposed to know. However, there are some factors that can be controlled, specifically pertaining to the method of education. Modern education seems to dictate, if some is good, more is better- more structure, more repetition, more homework, more tutoring and after school classes. This is what we have come to believe and expect. However, research suggests that "less is more" is a wise philosophy to adopt in this area.

According to Dr. Medlin, "Less intensive home school programs seemed to be related to higher achievement, as the amount of direct instruction provided by the parents, and the months per year of school were significantly negatively correlated with achievement. Giving grades for assignments and the frequent use of rewards for schoolwork were also significantly negatively related to SAT scores" (Medlin D. R., 1994).

This statement seems shocking and counter-intuitive for most. Why would a child, who drags their feet when expected to do anything educational, do better with less direct instruction and fewer incentives?

These results are not unique to homeschool children. A study of public-school children resulted in the following conclusion: "The pattern of data obtained indicated that, as predicted, the pressure induction interacted with level of controlling strategies used by teachers to affect student performance. More specifically, performance impairment was evidenced when children were taught by pressured teachers who used controlling strategies and the absence of choice options. Similarly, given the pressure manipulation, when teacher and student feelings of tension (shown in previous studies to covary with controlling behaviors) were combined with teacher behaviors (control and the absence of choice), students' performance deteriorated" (Cheryl Flink, 1990).

Higher stress, fewer choices, and less control over the learning material all resulted in poorer performance by students, compared to those who were under less stress and had more control over their learning experiences. According to scientists, this is because of intrinsic motivation- the drive to do something that is interesting or exciting, simply for the joy of doing it (Brian D Ray, 2000).

According to the research of Dr Brian Ray, children seek out challenges to overcome, simply for the satisfaction of overcoming them on their own. This tendency promotes self-confidence, independence, problem solving, creativity, and a sense of accomplishment. However, when that self-determination is jeopardized, and constraints or measures are put on them in the forms of time limits, parameters, or letter grades, that intrinsic motivation becomes threatened.

Many homeschool parents choose to teach their own children because they want to foster curiosity in them and provide opportunities to explore on their own. This means that homeschooling, by nature, caters to that intrinsic motivation much more. Perhaps, that is the real reason why homeschool students are often more self-motivated than those who go to public school. It is not that they are more disciplined, but rather that they have been given the opportunity to explore on their own, and have learned from an early age to ask questions and to seek out the information that they want to know.

Self-motivation means seeing the value in knowledge and craving it. It means identifying topics of interest and seeking out information on those subjects. Self-motivated students are interested in what they are learning, so they pursue it on their own and they remember it. For the self-motivated student, learning is its own reward.

Social Intelligence

The topic of socialization for students has been a big focus of concern and debate over the years. Despite the fact that many studies have demonstrated that homeschoolers seem to be on par or more socially intelligent than their public-school peers (Brian D. Ray, 2021), there seems to be a big disconnect here between perception and reality. Dr. Richard Medlin had this to say about it:

"A survey of public-school superintendents found that 92% believed homeschooled children do not receive adequate socialization experiences (Mayberry, Knowles, Ray & Marlow, 1995)… And a study of parents whose children attended public schools reported that 61% believed homeschooled children were isolated (Gray, 1993). One participant described the "majority" of homeschooled children as "socially handicapped"…

"In fact, [homeschool parents] are strongly committed to

providing positive socialization experiences for their children

(Gray, 1993; Gustafson, 1988; Howell, 1989; Martin, 1997;

Mayberry, 1989; Mayberry et al., 1995; Van Galen, 1987; Van

Galen & Pitman, 1991). They believe, however, that "socialization

is best achieved in an age-integrated setting under the auspices of

the family" (Tillman, 1995, p. 5), rather than in a conventional

school with its "unnatural" age segregation (Smedley, 1992, p. 13)

and institutional culture. Consequently, they make sure that their

children regularly take part in a variety of social activities

(Delahooke, 1986; Rakestraw, 1988; Ray, 1990, 1997, 2000, 2003;

Rudner, 1999; Wartes, 1988, 1990). These activities are

purposefully chosen to help children develop leadership abilities

and social skills in a positive, affirming environment (Johnson,

1991; Montgomery; 1989). "The perception of homeschooled

students as being isolated, uninvolved, and protected from peer

contact," therefore, "is simply not supported by the data"

(Montgomery, 1989, p. 9). Nevertheless, the social world of

homeschooled children is not the same as that of children attending

conventional schools (Chatham-Carpenter, 1994)" (Medlin R. G.,

2007).

Dr. Medlin's results were consistent with those of the study

conducted by Dr Ray. However, Dr. Medlin also highlighted some

important insights. The first, is in regard to the misconception that

homeschoolers are not afforded opportunities to socialize; the

second, recognizes the contrasting socialization strategies, which

may be part of the reason for the first result.

Whether intentionally or not, many homeschoolers seem to

support Albert Bandura's Social Learning Theory- the idea that

children learn from their environments and imitate the people in

them (McLeod, 2016). Because of this, many homeschoolers

prefer integrated environments that enforce the behaviors they

want to encourage- where older children can help younger children

while learning patience and leadership, and younger children learn

how to learn to imitate the behaviors of the older ones, while also learning that they matter. These relationships are fostered within families, as well as in group settings.

Many homeschool parents do not view classrooms full of children the same age as sufficient to learn these types of skills. On the contrary, a lot of children in public school struggle with negative self-worth, because of bullying and segregation. These issues are much less common in homeschool settings.

Social intelligence is important, because it plays a big role in individuals' success in life as they move on to careers and foster relationships outside of school. Ultimately, knowing how to take tests and fill out worksheets is not going to be an indicator of professional success, but leadership, problem-solving, collaboration, and critical thinking are all skills that are desired by employers, and encouraged in the homeschool environment. Teaching these skills at a young age, instead of starting in college, is much easier for the child, and also makes those skills seem much more intuitive in a workplace setting.

Independent Thinkers

One of the main differences between homeschooling and public schooling, is that homeschooling focuses more on the means-to-the-end instead of the end itself. It is less about knowing the right answer, and more about knowing how to find it. Many homeschoolers also take courses in logic and rhetoric, so they are able to form proper arguments and determine when a person's reasoning is emotional and manipulative, rather than based on sound logic.

The ability to think independently is an essential skill and a lost art. It is arguably as important as knowing how to count change; a person who is able to think independently is able to evaluate the information they are given for what it is, instead of taking the word of someone else. Someone who is unable to count change, can never know if they are being given the proper amount at the store; a person who is unable to calculate wages will never know if they are being paid what they have earned. For self-preservation and advancement, it is crucial for a person to be able to analyze information they are given, and investigate further. Since everyone is ultimately interested in their own well-being first, it is foolish to trust everyone blindly, without being able to determine the validity of what they say.

Homeschooling encourages students to draw their own conclusions from the material they are presented with, instead of memorizing someone else's interpretation. A reading assignment for history may turn into a study on the culture or worldview of the time, or how a person's religious beliefs may influence the decisions they make and ultimately shape the outcome. A homeschool family may discuss how the student's decision-making would be similar or different than the person they are studying, and why; they may discuss similarities between the time period they are learning about and the one they are living in. All of these ideas help to highlight the relevance of history, and to make it more memorable. Rather than simply memorizing facts to forget later, students are encouraged to identify with the person they are learning about, and to recognize the humanity of the figures they are studying. These activities encourage students to be actively engaged in the world around them, instead of simply being passive bystanders.

Independent thinkers are ground breakers. They find great satisfaction in inventing new ways to do things. They enjoy challenging the way things are done and finding more efficient ways to accomplish the task. They are resourceful, and find new applications for existing technologies. All new technologies and philosophies are discovered by independent thinkers.

Independent thinkers are coveted among employers. They make excellent leaders, because they are able to identify the problems that need to be addressed and they can figure out how to resolve them. Independent thinkers are more self-motivated, because they are guided by their own inquisition and hunger for knowledge and sense of accomplishment.

In a 2018 article by Forbes titled, "5 Ways To Become An Independent Thinker And Show Your Leadership," the author described independent thinkers as "refreshing" (Blank, 2018). The author's list of five items includes:

read- homeschoolers do a lot of reading, and some curricula (Charlotte Mason, et al.) focus heavily on reading.

Identify the other argument- a skill that is often developed during the high school years while learning logic and rhetoric. Some homeschoolers even implement Socratic seminars- an exercise which involves students arguing opposing positions of an issue for the purpose of hearing all sides and finding truth (classical education).

Interact with people who are different than you- this facet of homeschooling has already been addressed extensively.

Travel- some homeschool families choose to live in an RV and travel the country while teaching their kids on the road; others, plan their school year around family trips.

Focus on respect- this concept is also strongly emphasized through the integrative teaching that many homeschoolers experience in large families and through co-ops, as discussed before; also, through the use of Socratic seminars require respectful dialogue, even when there is disagreement.

The skills discussed above are learned from an early age in many homeschool families. Perhaps, this is why homeschool students tend to be very successful in continuing education and beyond. These are not skills that need to be developed intentionally as a way to further one's personal career, because they have already become habits by the time homeschoolers enter the workforce.

Well-Rounded Individuals

One of the primary goals of homeschooling is to raise up children to become well-rounded individuals. Individuals, who have been encouraged to grow academically, but also spiritually, emotionally, morally, and socially. Homeschool parents often encourage their children to step outside their comfort zones, if only for a minute, so they learn not to shy away from new and unfamiliar situations, but rather to take advantage of whatever opportunities they may present.

The ultimate goal is to build the child's self-confidence by teaching them that it is ok to fail or to not like something, but that by exploring the unknown it is possible to learn about the subject in question and about oneself. Exploring new ideas and concepts can help to discover unknown skills and passions, which is crucial for determining a course for continuing education and for future career prospects.

This tendency for homeschoolers to be very well-rounded, has caught the attention of many prominent figures, including Dr. Jay Lile, who wrote about it in his blog. He said,

"I first noticed this many years ago, when I employed a homeschool graduate to help me with certain research projects. At that time, she was studying genetics at the college she was attending. Despite being a "science geek," I found that I could have serious, in-depth discussion with her on topics like science, philosophy, Greek literature, opera, classical music, and politics. While I had gained knowledge of those areas over the course of a (then) 40-year lifespan, she was able to challenge me on all those topics (and more) despite being less than half my age" (Wile, 2010).

He has had many such experiences with homeschool students, and surmises that it is because the love of learning is not "socialized out of them." Instead of being made fun of for loving to learn, as many public-school students are by their less enthusiastic peers, homeschool students explore together and celebrate each other's achievements. This seems to be a very likely theory. Learning is much more fun when it is a social event in itself- when one is able to do it with friends who are equally enthusiastic, and able to celebrate with friends who share the same love for knowledge.

Encouraging students to pursue their interests produces a "go-getter" attitude, where they crave knowledge, and seek it with enthusiasm and gusto. It also results in skillsets as unique as they are, with many students double majoring in physics and music, or history and engineering. They are not limited by the parameters that society says make sense, but are limited only by their own interest and motivation. Homeschooling pursues a goal, but also celebrates the journey, and recognizes that the journey looks different for everyone.

Homeschooling emphasizes memorable experiences. It recognizes the value of trying new things and putting students in unpredictable situations. Children who are comfortable adapting to unexpected situations and talking to a variety of people become adults who can do the same. Successful maneuvering in numerous different environments builds confidence in the individual.

As students grow up and learn to adapt to the environment they live in, experiences in the "real world" help it all make more sense. They are better able to develop a good understanding of society and their place in it. Students who grow up experiencing the world feel like they have a place in it, and maybe they can make it better.

Homeschoolers celebrate knowledge as something to be collected and treasured, much the same way some people collect trading cards or trophies. Rather than a dull exercise that needs to be completed because it is a requirement, knowledge is its own reward and something to be pursued.

Homeschooling also recognizes the individuality of each student and their journey. Education is not one-size-fits-all, and students who are able to explore their own personal interests are much more likely to succeed and thrive. Homeschooling is not about isolating from the world, but rather about getting to know it

in one's own way. That is the secret to raising well-rounded

individuals.

Reasons for Homeschooling Summarized

There are a number of reasons why families decide to homeschool their children. Some families do it because it better compliments their lifestyle. If they move around a lot- out of necessity or by choice- homeschooling offers some much-needed consistency and flexibility.

Other families choose to homeschool for safety reasons. From school shootings to Tik Tok challenges, drugs to bullies and sexual predators, parents have an ever-growing number of reasons to question the safety of schools, and it has become clear that the "safety measures" put in place are not working. For many families, the most practical solution is to remove their children from the environment completely and keep them in a place of relative safety, where they have more control over the people their children are exposed to.

Some parents remove their children from school because they recognize more individualized needs and the benefit of more focused attention for the learning process. Rather than medicating their children to keep them still in their seats, these parents recognize their students need to move and explore, and they give them the freedom to do so. Many parents see the "assembly line" approach to education as detrimental to the mental, emotional, academic, and physical development of their child.

Many parents are also concerned with the inability of public schools to effectively teach basic skills such as reading and writing. More than just important life skills, these abilities play a crucial role in their success as adults. With studies showing that eighty-five percent of youth who interface with the juvenile court system are functionally low-literate (The Relationship Between Incarceration and Low Literacy, n.d.), parents are opting to take matters into their own hands and teach their own children, so their children can be better equipped and less likely to end up as a part of that statistic.

Perhaps one of the biggest reasons for homeschooling, is parents want to know exactly what their children are being taught. The past couple of years have been very eye-opening for a lot of people, as lockdowns and virtual learning meant that many parents heard things they never expected from their children's educators.

As school has become less focused on learning basic skills, and has expanded to include other topics that many parents see as unessential or inappropriate, many parents have opted to teach their own children, to ensure that they learn things they need to know to be successful, while omitting things that may not conform to their own ideology. Homeschooling allows families to incorporate lessons pertaining to their own culture or religion in ways that are not possible elsewhere (Ray, 2015).

Homeschooling looks different in every family. The methods are different, and the subject priorities are different. However, at its core is the desire to provide the best, most academically enriching, most encouraging and confidence-building environment possible for their child. These parents truly have their children's best interest at heart, and that is evident in the sacrifice that goes into the process.

Many homeschool families are single income families. This does not mean that they are wealthy or even middle class, it simply means that they have made home education a priority and have made sacrifices so it is possible. Cheryl Fields-Smith wrote a book telling the powerful stories of single black mothers who found a way to provide for their children and educate them, because they knew that education is essential, and because they didn't want their children to lose touch with their past and the truths of where they came from (Fields-Smith, 2020).

Homeschooling is an added expense. According to ThinkImpact.com, the cost of homeschooling is between $700-$1,800 per child annually (ThinkImpact.com, 2022), and though this is significantly less than the $15,000 annual taxpayer expense for public school students (Brian D. Ray, 2021), most states do not offer a tax break for parents who choose to homeschool their children (with the exception of Illinois, Louisiana, and Minnesota).

Utah and Colorado have a program called My Tech High, which provides some public funds to be allocated to homeschool parents for school supplies, field trips, and extracurricular activities, but neither of these options are available for the majority of the country. Nevertheless, homeschool families find ways to make it work, either by utilizing libraries in their area, sharing resources amongst themselves, or by some other method. Despite the financial limitations many families face, research still shows that homeschooled children score consistently above average on standardized tests, and they have above average rates of college graduation (Brian D. Ray, 2021).

In addition to being a monetary expense, homeschooling is also a major time commitment. Homeschool parents shop for their own curriculum, they create their own lesson plans, they plan their own field trips, gather materials, track attendance and course completion according to state laws, teach their students, and afterward help them apply for an appropriate college or trade school. It is not for the faint of heart, and many parents decide that it is not the right course for their families. However, a growing number of parents are willing to take on the challenge for the sake of ensuring that their children get the education they need to be successful.

Determine Your Homeschool Style

As with most things in life, the hardest part of homeschooling is getting started. Even once one has decided it is the right course for their family, it can be overwhelming to try and wade through all of the information and resources to determine what will work best. Understand that the homeschool process is one of trial and error and learning together. One does not have to go into it knowing everything. In fact, some of the most successful homeschoolers are those who recognize that they do not know it all, but are either willing to learn or determined to find someone who can do it better to help them.

This chapter will attempt to summarize the seven primary homeschool methods that families choose to use, while the following chapters will go into more depth on each one and provide resources for each. The purpose is to create a "cheat sheet" of sorts, to enable you to compare approaches and begin narrowing down the options you are interested in for your family. After examining them together, you will be able to delve into the methods that have the greatest appeal to you.

Classical education focuses on teaching students to think for themselves. There are three main phases of the education process- grammar, logic, and rhetoric, and the end goal is for students to be able to, not only formulate their own opinions, but also to support them in a debate setting in an articulate way. Classical education teaches primarily from a Christian worldview, but also hearkens back to the roots of education by teaching Latin and Greek/Roman mythology, often with some time devoted to classical music and art history.

Unit Study homeschool programs focus the different learning avenues around a central topic of interest. For a predetermined period of time, assignments and activities are chosen to help the student understand a specific subject. At the end of the timeframe given, a new topic is chosen and new assignments that are related to the new topic. Unit study curricula can be purchased as a kit, or compiled by the parent for the student's specific interests.

Montessori education is used predominantly in the early years, and centers around five key components: individual work, freedom to work at one's own pace, sensory learning, self-directed study, and a peaceful environment. A great option for more tactile learners, Montessori provides resources and opportunities for personal exploration and creative play. This school style makes available a wide range of stimuli to inspire students' creativity- things such as wooden blocks, musical instruments, sandboxes, bean and rice buckets, and finger paints.

Waldorf education focuses on the arts as an essential tool for teaching and touching a person's "spirit." The Waldorf approach uses very few textbooks, and instead relies on literary arts- poetry, fairy tales, myths, and songs to teach truth and morality to students.

Charlotte Mason homeschool curriculum begins with the premise that all children are people. That they are all equipped with the same basic tools for learning, regardless of social status, and have their own opinions and preferences. It is very literature-driven, but also emphasizes the importance of free-play and time outside, as well as developing an appreciation for music and art. The goal of Charlotte Mason is to develop the whole person through a variety of different practices, while also respecting the individuality of each student, and giving them room to grow into their own unique person.

Multiple Intelligences methodology recognizes seven intelligence "types": visual/spatial, verbal/linguistic, logical/mathematical, bodily/kinesthetic, musical/rhythmic, interpersonal, and intrapersonal. It works to identify the strengths of the individual student, and then teaches the way they learn best. This method seeks to build self-confidence through ease-of-learning.

Relaxed/Eclectic homeschooling does not strictly adhere to any specific method of homeschooling, but mixes and matches pieces of different methods to suit the needs/desires of the family. Rather than firmly committing to one method of schooling, families have the freedom to choose their favorite parts of a variety of different curricula to make a learning program that is uniquely their own. This can even include dedicating time to one's own culture or family history.

Unschooling gives students the freedom to learn organically through exploration and play. It is mostly hands-off, and trusts that children will learn what they need to on their own through their own curiosity-driven discovery. There is very little formal learning that happens, and very little structure.

By now it should be very clear that homeschool approaches to education vary greatly, and they are all different than public school methodologies. Homeschool families have much more flexibility due to smaller class sizes, and have a much more personal interest in the success of their students. These factors contribute to the overall higher success rates of homeschoolers.

While it is true that a more individualized approach is easier for students and produces better outcomes, for those who have gone to public school for a while the transition can be very difficult at first. For this reason, a period of "deschooling" is often helpful. This will be discussed in a later chapter.

Classical Homeschool

"Classical education is based on models of learning that go back to the Middle Ages, although its earliest roots lie in the Greek and Roman civilizations. Dorothy Sayers was one of a number of scholars who re-popularized this method of learning in the twentieth century. Classical education challenges the vocational orientation of most modern education by instead concentrating on learning that forms the inner person—their character and virtues. At the same time, classical students learn how to think, how to learn independently, and how to present their own ideas—all of which ultimately prepares them for a wide range of vocations" (Cathy Duffy, 2021).

Classical education consists of many of the subjects that people are used to associating with "school." It is often textbook based, though not exclusively. In this way, it has some similarities to traditional education. However, Classical education is probably more comparable to the education the founding fathers would have received, rather than modern day public schoolers.

Classical education goes beyond what modern schools teach, and also exposes students to the roots of education and our modern-day society. By introducing them to Latin, to famous literary works by people such as Plato, Hippocrates, Aristotle, and others, and by showing them the ways these topics influence our culture today, students are allowed to develop a better understanding of why current ideologies exist.

Classical education embraces the wisdom of the past and recognizes the continuity of time- how modern society is not independent from the ideas of the past, but rather is derived from them. Classical education suggests that truly great works of literature, art, and music connect with people across generations; it looks to the past for a better understanding of who we are as individuals and as members of the human race.

Classical education consists of three basic stages from elementary school through high school- Grammar, Logic, and Rhetoric. Elementary school is the Grammar stage. It sets the foundation for learning that will be expanded on in the future. It focuses primarily on the core subjects, such as math, reading, writing, history, and science. The grammar stage gives students the basic tools that they need to participate in the world they live in.

The Logic stage begins around middle school, and it starts to build on the foundation that was laid in the Grammar years. Logic is often taught as a class during this time, and it is used to train students to create valid arguments and to recognize statements that are manipulative and not grounded in facts. During the logic phase, students are taught to make connections, and to start looking at things comparatively instead of as isolated subjects.

In high school, this learning is expanded further during the Rhetoric phase. In this phase, students learn to develop and defend their own ideas using the logic they learned previously. Students may also be taught worldview, government, and about church history and denominations.

The rhetoric phase of classical education celebrates the differences of opinion that people hold and their ability to argue intelligently and respectfully about their differing views. This is often done through the use of Socratic seminars- group discussions where students take turns arguing opposing views amongst themselves in an attempt to find truth.

Classical education argues that truth is not found at either end of a spectrum, but somewhere in the middle, and it is through respectful dialogue of opposing views that individuals can arrive at the truth of a matter. So, classical education develops a love for truth and the pursuit of it. Not simply accepting as truth what one is told, but by looking at history and current information, and by intelligent discussion with those who hold opposing viewpoints. It teaches students to be confident in their own deductions, and to be comfortable disagreeing with those around them.

Below are some top-rated Classical curriculum programs:

1. **Memoria Press** – Sells all-inclusive curriculum packages for each year, K-12, or provides an online school that parents can utilize. They supply curriculum for private schools throughout the country, and also have a special needs curriculum. Memoria Press also has its own forum and podcast. More information is available at www.memoriapress.com.

2. **Classical Academic Press** – Sells all-inclusive curriculum packages through seventh grade. The high school curriculum has course options to choose from, much like college. In addition to their curriculum, they also have online course options, teacher training, homeschool coops, and an education blog. They supply curricula to public and charter schools around the country, as well. More information is available at www.classicalacademicpress.com.

3. **Veritas Press** – Offers all-inclusive curriculum packages with three different levels- good, better, best- depending on how much help a parent wants with the homeschooling process. They also offer online live and self-paced courses. More information can be found at www.veritaspress.com.

4. **The Good and the Beautiful** – offers course-specific curriculum sets for grades K-8, as well as supplemental resources that many homeschool parents find useful for their homeschool journey. This program is very well liked as a way to enhance something that a family is already doing. More information can be found at www.goodandbeautiful.com.

5. **Classical Conversations** – is a community-based educational program. Children learn together in an interactive and engaging environment. Parents act as mentors as the students work through the program together, which is organized by age instead of by grade. There is a

search option to find groups in your local community on the website: www.classicalconversations.com.

6. **Well-Trained Mind Academy** – is an online classical education program for grades 5-12. They offer semester and year-long courses for students that are live or recorded, and they also offer tutoring. Parents can find more information at: www.wtmacademy.com.

There are a number of other classical curriculum options out there, as well, but these are some of the top-rated ones. If you think classical education is your preferred option, you can use this as a starting point as you search for the right curriculum for your family.

Unit Study Homeschool

Unit study homeschool teaches students by assigning course work and activities related to a central theme. The topic can be a favorite book, a science experiment, historical event or place, or other subject of interest. This kind of homeschooling is especially helpful for learning about time periods throughout history or geographic regions. Parents may incorporate food, clothing, games, or music that is unique to the time or place they are learning about, giving them a more hands-on and memorable immersion experience. Typically, a unit study on a particular subject lasts for one to two weeks.

The goal of the unit study approach is to fill in the gaps that sometimes exist with the textbook approach to learning. Instead of memorizing information that does not seem to have any relevance, the unit study attempts to bring life and meaning to the material.

Parents sometimes choose to create their own curriculum, or there are numerous unit study style curriculum options that may include books, lesson plans, work pages, activities, field trip suggestions, science kits, and more. Unit study curricula do not typically have a virtual learning option, but some have online resources. Unit study learning programs are designed to provide the materials and instructions to empower parents to step into the "teacher" role easily, rather than delegating to another person or online platform, though unit studies are sometimes done in a group/co-op setting.

Below is a list of some popular unit study curricula. It is not a comprehensive list, but can serve as a guide while examining different curriculum options.

Literature Centric Unit Study

Five in a Row- is a curriculum for Preschool-6th grade. It focuses on teaching social studies, art, applied math, science, and language through books, follow-up questions, and activities. (https://fiveinarow.com)

Beautiful Feet- is a history-centric unit study curriculum for K-12th grade. The goal of the curriculum is to create a memorable school experience for children and meaningful interactions for families. (https://www.bfbooks.com/)

Book Shark- is a secular homeschool unit study curriculum for PreK-12th grade that is organized by levels instead of grades, so students feel more freedom to move at their own pace. Curriculum is available as individual subjects or as a bundle, and focuses primarily on history, language arts, science, math, spelling, and handwriting. (https://www.bookshark.com)

Classical Centric Unit Study

Tapestry of Grace- Is a unit study curriculum that offers twelve different subjects at four different difficulty levels. The goal of this program is to help students see "the patterns of God's personality and works" throughout history. Tapestry of Grace contains elements of classical and Charlotte Mason education methods. (https://tapestryofgrace.com)

Geography Centric Unit Study

Geo Matters- is a unit study that focuses on geography, and the movements of people and civilizations throughout history. It is a K-8 curriculum that incorporates everything except math using an integrated approach to learning. It utilizes elements of Charlotte Mason education methods, as well as others, to create an engaging and memorable school experience. (https://geomatters.com)

Character Trait Centric Unit Study

Konos- is a unit study approach that focuses on positive character traits as the basis for month-long unit studies for elementary and high school. Konos focuses on the five D's for learning: Do, Discover, Dramatize, Dialogue, Drill. (https://konos.com)

Themed Unit Studies

Winter Promise- is an "a la carte" style unit study approach that pulls from a variety of techniques. In addition to having theme options for students for core subjects, it incorporates elements of Charlotte Mason and Multiple Intelligences, as well as family activities, to create a unique experience with lots of variety. For PreK-12th grade. (https://winterpromise.com)

Montessori Education

"We cannot know the consequences of suppressing a child's spontaneity when he is just beginning to be active. We may even suffocate life itself. That humanity which is revealed in all its intellectual splendor during the sweet and tender age of childhood should be respected with a kind of religious veneration. It is like the sun which appears at dawn or a flower just beginning to bloom. Education cannot be effective unless it helps a child to open up himself to life." – Maria Montessori

The Montessori learning system was designed by Maria Montessori, a physician and anthropologist, in 1929. It is a learning program for children from birth to twelve-years-old that stresses the importance of independent play and discovery for the development, satisfaction, and self-esteem of the child. It stresses the importance of experiential learning for creating a deeper understanding of math, language arts, music, science, and social interactions.

The Montessori classroom environment is thoughtfully designed with age-appropriate activities. The core program is secular, and provides opportunities for students to explore their own unique interests at their own pace. Activities within the classroom setting are largely unrestricted unless they present a danger to the student or their peers.

There are three main age groups for the Montessori teaching strategy: the toddler years (0-3), primary years (3-6), and elementary years (6-12). Each level offers more complex activities for motor skills development, problem solving and collaboration, and discovering their own personal interests and abilities. Some common toys and activities present in a Montessori classroom include blocks, pegs, puzzles, musical instruments, paints, Pikler triangles, foam squares, sensory bins, and more! Outside play is also highly encouraged. Some people also include a "farm school" experience for older children (12-15 years), for real-world exposure to the importance of hard work and dependability, business management, good stewardship, and the fundamental knowledge of where food comes from.

The guiding principles of Montessori are as follows: respect for children and allowing them to control their own learning experience, a prepared environment complete with age-appropriate activities to encourage exploration and growth, hands-on, "whole self" learning, independent discovery, imagination that is promoted through open-ended activities, freedom of choice within reasonable boundaries, and the opportunity to work things out independently.

The Montessori method stresses the importance of an environment of learning- an environment that is safe, exciting, and inspires children to want to pursue their interests. The ultimate goal is to raise children to love learning for the adventure it can be, and to train them to be self-motivated (Montessori Northwest, n.d.).

The Montessori education strategy works well on its own or as a compliment to other methods. Many homeschool families create a Montessori environment for their children in the toddler and preschool years, and then transition to other forms of learning when they deem it appropriate. Similarly, parents who opt not to use it as their primary schooling method, still use elements of Montessori education in their home- choosing open-play type toys and creative activities to add variety and stimulation during recess and free time.

Whether formally included or a happy coincidence, many homeschool families do recognize the importance of play for young children, and strive to allow their bodies and minds to run wild. It is not always a designated schoolroom full of toys that fit the description, but many families are more selective about the toys that are purchased for Christmas and birthdays because they recognize the value of open play and toys that facilitate creativity.

Montessori Curriculum Options

Allison's Montessori – Is a great one-stop shop for all things Montessori. They offer materials bundles for classrooms, curriculum bundles through upper elementary years, and additional resources for those looking for a little extra guidance. (https://www.alisonsmontessori.com)

Montessori Services – Makes a wide variety of authentic Montessori materials, many of which are made in the USA of non-toxic materials. They also offer curriculum bundles, and resources for parents who are looking for additional help. (https://www.montessoriservices.com)

North American Montessori Center – Is rated among the best, most user-friendly Montessori curriculum options available. They offer curriculum options for infants through age twelve, help manuals for teachers and parents, and additional training resources on USB or DVD. (https://www.montessoritraining.net)

Waldorf Education

"The heart of the Waldorf method is that education is an art-it must speak to the child's experience. To educate the whole child, his heart and his will must be reached, as well as the mind."
– Rudolf Steiner

The central premise of Waldorf education is that human beings exist and operate within three spheres- the head, the heart, and the will. The goal is to engage the whole student. It is traditionally a secular program, and recognizes the importance of engaging the head and the heart in the process of education, and allowing the individual some room to influence the direction of their learning. Without the engagement of any one piece of the whole child, there will be an imbalance, and optimal learning will not occur. Waldorf education focuses on learning through social interactions and artistic engagement. It uses dance, movement, stories, music, and other creative outlets to connect with students and to help them connect to their world. "Throughout the grades, we are concerned with the development of the child's capacities: academic capacities, capacities of love and compassion, and the capacities to fulfill one's destiny" (Seifert, n.d.).

Rudolf Steiner, the founder of the Waldorf method of learning, believed that each person has one or two temperaments that are dominant: choleric- intense and fast-acting and easily frustrated, phlegmatic- slow and steady and content by themselves, melancholic- slow paced and more pessimistic or easily discouraged, and sanguine- energetic and social, often struggling to concentrate on a given task. Because of these variations in temperament, in a classroom setting lessons are often taught three or four different ways so that each student is taught in a way that they can identify with and that motivates them (Mesrobian, 2021).

Waldorf education occurs in three main phases. The first one, from birth to age seven, consists primarily of free play and exploration. It is the part of the child's life when they are learning about their environment and how to manipulate it to their liking. These years consist of little, if any, formal education, and instead this time is spent cultivating the physical skills of the student, often within social experiences.

Once children are able to think in terms of allegory they advance to the second phase of Waldorf learning- from about age seven to fourteen. During this phase, literature, poetry, music, and art are used a great deal to teach morals, life lessons, and about the world. Students are encouraged to identify with characters in the stories, and imagine what they would do in similar situations. There is an emphasis on connecting with the "divine spark"- that part of each individual that makes them uniquely themself, and students are taught to look inward as well as outward- to understand themselves as much as they do the world around them- and to express their feelings through music, art, movement, and the written word. Teachers are taught to connect with each of their students individually, and to teach the lesson in a way that the individual child will be able to relate to.

During adolescence, ages fourteen to twenty-one, students are given increased autonomy over their learning experience, and are taught to think critically about issues they are presented with. Instead of the emphasis on teaching morality through fairy tales, this third phase of the Waldorf curriculum gives students the tools to make their own judgments about the world, and exercise their own discernment.

Waldorf education attempts to keep learning lighthearted and fun with stories of far off and mystical places while also grounding students with a sense of morality. It is, arguably, the teaching approach that requires the most emotional involvement from the teacher, and is challenging in that it requires a certain amount of psychological analysis in order to understand and speak to the child in a much more personal way. This element of Waldorf education can be easier for homeschool parents, who by nature know their children much more intimately than teachers at a school are able. It focuses on connection, freedom of expression, and the beauty of creativity.

Waldorf Curriculum Options

Lavender Blue- Waldorf curriculum and quick start guide for new homeschoolers (https://www.lavendersbluehomeschool.com/)

Oak Meadow- A Waldorf-inspired homeschool curriculum that has been modified to more closely resemble public school curriculum and ease the transition to a new learning style (https://www.oakmeadow.com/)

Waldorf Essentials – Curriculum and training options for new homeschool families who are interested in the Waldorf teaching method (https://www.waldorfessentials.com/waldorfhomeschool)

Waldorfish- Offers e-courses and online resources for homeschoolers and charter schools to make this art-based curriculum more easily available to students

(https://waldorfish.com)

Charlotte Mason Homeschool

We do not merely give a religious education because that would seem to imply the possibility of some other education, a secular education, for example. But we hold that all education is divine, that every good gift of knowledge and insight comes from above, that the Lord the Holy Spirit is the supreme educator of mankind, and that the culmination of all education (which may at the same time be reached by a little child) is that personal knowledge of an intimacy with God in which our being finds its fullest perfection – Charlotte Mason

Charlotte Mason's philosophy on education consists of twenty principles (Laurio, 2004). These principles focus on the identity of children as people- born with personalities and preferences, rather than just a blank slate to fill as some suggest. She taught that children are not born good or evil, but are capable of becoming either one, depending on the influences they are

exposed to. She also taught that learning should be organic and

child-driven. She believed that the only true education is self-

education, and teachers' primary responsibilities are to teach

discipline and self-control and to expose the children to as many

opportunities for learning as possible; that each child will soak up

and remember the nuggets of knowledge that are relevant to them,

according to the gifting and direction they receive from the Divine

Spirit.

Rather than separating education and religion, Charlotte

Mason taught that education is very much influenced by the

workings of the Spirit in children's lives, and teachers should not

only show children the world and point to the Creator's hand in its

orchestration, but they should also allow space for the Spirit to

work in the lives of each individual child uniquely in the midst of

the education process.

Rather than lectures that tell students what to think,

Charlotte Mason's methods involve reading copious "living

books"- books that bring stories or events to life for the child- and allowing the child time to reflect on the material read and form their own opinions of it. It involves copying or reciting favorite passages, playing outside, dabbling in the arts, and collecting as many experiences as possible. In this way, the children are able to take ownership of their learning, and pursue knowledge for the genuine love of finding their own special "treasures." This approach to learning develops confident and self-motivated students, a depth of understanding beyond simple textbook work, and numerous ways to connect to the world and the people around them.

Charlotte Mason's method teaches that introducing children to a wide range of topics will better help them to find their unique gifts and passions. Every child is distinctive, and their interpretations of material and the connections they make will vary greatly from one to another. So, the best thing a parent or educator can do is provide thought-provoking experiences for the child to wrestle with and interpret based on the things they know from life and from their books. When children are given these tools in the context of a relationship with God, the Spirit speaks to the child's heart, and nudges them in the direction they are meant to go.

The Charlotte Mason method emphasizes intentional and meaningful work. Busy work is a waste of time, and does not contribute much to the mind of a child, but thoughtful exercises that develop skills, in addition to stimulating the mind, bring great satisfaction and depth to the child.

Charlotte Mason's methods include reading the best quality books available- timeless classics and new treasures- to provide a better understanding of old and new ideas. The reading selections should be narrated, because a story that can be told is a story that is understood. Favorite selections are carefully written or practiced and recited- every piece intentional, meaningful, and exciting in its own way.

Charlotte Mason was a big advocate for allowing children to grow into the space they are meant to fill, rather than simplifying the world in a way that makes the real world seem big and scary and foreign. She saw the potential in children, and understood their ability to rise to the task of navigating and interpreting the real world for what it is, without requiring it to be watered down.

The Charlotte Mason method encourages awe in the wonders of creation. It teaches children to stop and smell the flowers, to admire the butterflies, to help things grow- to appreciate the little things and marvel at the little miracles that surround them every day. It teaches them to love the beautiful things in the world, and to do their part to help preserve them.

There are several different curriculum options that have been developed based on Charlotte Mason's approach to teaching. Some of the more popular ones are listed below:

Charlotte Mason Curriculum Options

Ambleside Online – Free online curriculum that consists of book lists, narration, copywork, and "riches" (composer study, art study, folk songs, hymns) on rotation. Forum and additional resources available for parents. www.amblesideonline.org

The Good and the Beautiful - Charlotte Mason- inspired curriculum available by subject, as well as a free book list. (https://www.goodandbeautiful.com/)

My Father's World- Charlotte Mason- inspired curriculum available by subject through eighth grade, as well as an online community and resources for parents. (https://www.mfwbooks.com)

A Gentle Feast- A Charlotte Mason- inspired curriculum developed on a four-year rotation and sold as yearly bundles. Teacher planner and other resources also available for purchase. Two weeks free to try before buying the full curriculum. (https://agentlefeast.com/)

Heart of Dakota- A Charlotte Mason- inspired curriculum centered around "living books" and unit study- type activities. Available by subject with options for each level. Community resources also available. (https://heartofdakota.com/)

Multiple Intelligences Homeschool

The Multiple Intelligences Theory was developed by Howard Gardner in 1983, and hinges on the idea that everyone is smart in their own way and learns according to their own unique abilities. According to this theory, there are eight separate ways that people process information, and most people are exceptionally good at two or three. The Multiple Intelligences Theory argues that the best way to teach people is by recognizing their strengths and teaching to those abilities. The eight "intelligences" are: verbal-linguistic (word smart), logical-mathematical (logic smart), visual-spatial (picture smart), auditory-musical (music smart), bodily-kinesthetic (body smart), interpersonal (people smart), intrapersonal (self-smart), and naturalistic (nature smart) (Connections Academy, 2021).

People with linguistic intelligence are good at understanding words and are able to articulate well. They understand language and its function, and are able to use it to achieve an end goal. They often end up in career fields that relate to written or oral communication.

A person with logical intelligence is primarily left brained, and is able to analyze information logically. They are good problem solvers, see patterns, like numbers and science, and are often asking "why." They often choose a career in accounting, research, mathematics, engineering, computer analysis, or another related field.

If a person has spatial intelligence, or picture smarts, they are good at using and manipulating space. They are able to scale their project to fit within the parameters of their workspace. Sculptors, interior designers, architects, and graphic designers all have good spatial intelligence.

Bodily-kinesthetic intelligence, or "body smarts," is the ability to move or use one's body to create art or solve problems.

Dancers, athletes, physical therapists, acrobats, carpenters, and mechanics tend to be more "body smart."

A person who has musical intelligence, or "music smarts," is skilled at understanding the ebbs and flows of music, and the components of great composition or performance. They often work in the music industry in some capacity, either as a teacher, performer, composer, DJ, or producer.

Interpersonal intelligence is "people smarts," or the ability to understand peoples' meanings, intentions, motivations, or moods. They often end up working in sales, management, public relations, psychology, or other related fields.

If a person has intrapersonal intelligence (self smarts), they understand their own personal strengths, weaknesses, fears, motivators, and goals, and they use these things to regulate their own life. These people are able to use their insights to help others, and often become a clergy member, counselor, therapist, or an entrepreneur.

People who have naturalist intelligence (nature smarts), have a love and intuitive understanding of the natural world. They are able to identify elements that go unnoticed by most people, and may get a career in the natural sciences- Geology, Botany, Astronomy, Biology, etc.

The multiple intelligences method of schooling looks at a child's strengths and interests and attempts to teach to those things. So, a child who shows signs of logical intelligence will focus on math problems and logic puzzles, while spending less time studying art. A child who is nature smart may read more Natural Geographic magazines and fewer fiction novels. In this way, children are able to learn in an easier, and more enjoyable way. One of the biggest arguments for this kind of teaching points out that ease-of-learning builds self-confidence in children, which in turn makes learning easier. (A child who finds learning tedious and hard is more likely to stop trying.) By taking time to learn about the individual child and take their unique interests and learning styles into consideration, parents can make the learning process easier on everyone.

This kind of education is almost impossible in a public school setting, but is very achievable at home. Simply from a logistics standpoint, even the best, most dedicated teacher has limitations due to the sheer number of students they have to instruct every day. Children at home are able to have a much more individualized experience, and for many homeschool families, the Multiple Intelligences style of teaching is present to some degree in their home education program.

There are a lot of simple ways to create a customized learning experience for children. Tools such as audio books for auditory learners, counting tools for hands-on learners, or exercises that involve movement for kinesthetic learners go a long way toward keeping children engaged and confident in their abilities. Confidence is possibly one of the most underrated tools in modern education, because a child who is confident will be more engaged and more willing to try. A child's confidence, or lack of confidence, feeds a cycle toward curiosity and learning, or one toward disengagement and timidity. Teaching toward a child's strengths is a great way to help them reach their full potential.

Relaxed/Eclectic Homeschool

Relaxed, or eclectic, homeschooling simply means that parents exercise their right to pick and choose elements of different curricula that they feel are best suited to their families' needs, instead of sticking religiously to one curriculum or method of teaching. A family who teaches eclectically may choose to use The Good and the Beautiful, a Charlotte Mason-based curriculum, for literature, while using Beautiful Feet, a history-centric unit study, for history and writing. They may choose to teach Latin, which is more common with a Classical education approach, and may also elect to do special science classes at the local children's museum.

The benefit of the eclectic homeschool method is it is highly individualized, and it can take into consideration the unique interests of the child. It can also be very adaptive, so children are able to take advantage of field trip opportunities, or schoolwork can be modified to incorporate family trips and other unique experiences as they come along.

This exercise of re-evaluating and making changes is a good life skill to possess, and it is one that children benefit from seeing. Not everything is black and white- sometimes, decisions are simply picking a strategy for advancement. This is very much the case with homeschooling- there is not necessarily a right or wrong way to do it, but there may be a better way for one's own family. Because of this, there is nothing wrong with trying a curriculum in one subject for a year and then switching to another if the first one does not seem to resonate with the child, or if it is hard for the parent to teach.

Eclectic homeschooling is like making selections from a buffet. There aren't necessarily wrong choices one can make, but some options may be better than others. In the case of homeschool curriculum, this mainly has to do with teaching and learning styles and family dynamic. A good choice for a family is a piece of curriculum that makes sense to everyone and is enjoyable to work through; a poorer choice is something that is hard to understand or unpleasant to get through. If a child tries a workbook for a year and always dreads that specific part of their school day more than the rest, then that workbook might be something to look at replacing the following year. It does not mean replacing the entire curriculum if it seems to work well for the most part, it simply means looking at each piece individually and finding ways to make the learning process as easy and exciting as possible.

Eclectic/relaxed homeschooling is a great strategy for families who want their school experience to be vibrant and flexible. It reflects the natural ebb and flow and unpredictable nature of life, and tries to make the most of the opportunities that come along. Eclectic homeschooling looks for ways to make learning a part of everyday life, and life full of engaging ways to learn.

The homeschool process is a journey that involves learning for the entire family, and it is not uncommon for new homeschool families to choose a curriculum bundle that they like to get started, because it is a simple way to make sure nothing is missed. Then, once they have adjusted to the process of home learning, many families adopt more of an eclectic schooling style- replacing pieces of the curriculum they like less well with other things that are better suited to their families' needs. This becomes especially true when dealing with children who learn in a unique way, as in the case of dyslexia, ADHD, etc, which will be discussed in later chapters.

Eclectic homeschooling embraces individuality and change, and looks for ways to enhance the opportunities that are already being taken advantage of. It can have as much or little structure as a family chooses to adhere to, but reflects the empowerment of being able to look at possibilities with an open mind and craft a unique experience for one's children based on local prospects and family values. Eclectic/relaxed homeschooling sees the benefit of a variety of experiences and recognizes that life very rarely happens exactly as we plan it. It is a strategy that, for many, forms with time as parents become aware of all of the possibilities. As parents' confidence grows in their ability to teach, they are empowered to

make changes for the benefit of their family.

Unschooling

One of the first, and perhaps one of the hardest concepts that parents struggle to comprehend when taking on the task of homeschooling, is that learning does not have to happen in a classroom setting, and it does not even happen best in that environment. Education is an end that we strive for, but the means to that end does not matter.

There are recommendations for what a child should know by a certain age, but even these are flexible as every child learns differently. Families who understand this concept find the process of homeschooling to be much more enjoyable and less stressful. No one is watching over a parent's shoulder to observe how they teach; and follow up that happens is simply to make sure that children are being taught and they are learning.

The homeschool style with the least structure is known as "unschooling," and it simply means that children learn from their environment, play, and real-life experiences instead of book work. Unschooling encourages free play, imagination, exploration, curiosity, and personal initiative in finding out how to do things.

Families who use an unschooling method of homeschooling often take road trips for extended periods of time, and read books about the places they visit along the way. They may spend long periods of time outside, play copious amounts of Legos, frequent museums, and pass their days exploring topics that are of interest to them. Most unschooled families use very few workbooks or true curriculum books, and instead stick to literature and non-fiction books about their interests. Children who are taught in this way are often very curious and self-motivated because the topics they study are those that they want to learn about.

Unschooled students have a lot of control over the direction of their education, which can potentially make their journey a very natural progression to choosing a career field. By learning about things that interest them, they also learn about themselves and the subjects that they are passionate about. If passion and talent intersect at any point, it is a topic that warrants more thorough investigation.

Some parents prefer to maintain some control over the direction of their students' learning, so that students will continue to push themselves beyond their comfort zones and explore possibilities they may not have considered, but that is also one of the benefits of field trips for the curious mind.

Most students find field trips and other outings to be stimulating and very memorable, especially because they are able to learn through many different channels at once. Field trips often include visual, auditory, and tactile stimulation, as well as opportunities to engage and ask questions. Environments of this kind, that promote engaged learning through many different channels, are the places where the most memorable learning happens, and homes that provide space for children to take ownership of their education and enjoy it tend to have a much smoother learning experience.

Education does not have to be the laborious ordeal that most people think of it as. Public schools as they are now are a fairly new concept that was refined around the time of the industrial revolution. Education was industrialized to accommodate the changing needs of the workforce of the time, but in a lot of ways this one-size-fits-all approach to learning has taken the humanity out of education, and turned it into something that many people despise.

People are not machines. Despite the arguments that some try to make, individuals are born with an innate desire to control their own destiny, and there is fulfillment in being able to take ownership of the learning process and explore new ideas previously unknown.

Unschooling embraces this facet of humanity, this desire to choose one's own, uncharted path and follow it wherever it may lead. It recognizes that true and memorable learning happens when a person is doing it to quench their own insatiable curiosity, not because there is an obligation that needs to be fulfilled. It celebrates learning that is organic and driven by personal curiosity.

Knowledge of this kind is its own reward.

Deschooling after Public Education

Children who switch from public school to homeschool often have a very hard time transitioning from one to the other. Most of them are burned out and have learned to hate school after years of being fed stagnant information to memorize for tests. New homeschool parents often find that it is an endless battle to get their children to engage with the new curriculum or participate in the activities they are assigned. When parent and child are thrown into a new education style after having already been jaded by the previous one, it can be nearly impossible to successfully navigate the rocky waves that come with trying to recalibrate life in such a dramatic way.

For families who find themselves in this situation, a period of deschooling can be very beneficial. "Deschooling" simply means taking a step back- a break. It means allowing time to decompress and recover from the stress of the performance-centered public education style. During this time, families may take trips together or visit museums of interest, but formal education is not attempted until the family is ready to begin enjoying education.

A lot of people think it is counterintuitive to stop school completely for a period of time. After all, most people have been taught that taking a break means falling behind. But, this is where "work smarter, not harder" really comes into play. Children who are actively engaged in the learning process and are taught the way they learn best tend to learn much faster than those who are fulfilling an obligation.

This is a major reason why homeschoolers' school days may only last two or three hours; it is not that they learn less, it is that they learn more efficiently than their public-schooled peers. Allowing children some time to let go of some of the hate they feel toward education, means that they are more open to learning that is enjoyable to them, and if they can learn to enjoy the education process, it is much easier for everyone.

Deschooling can look like unschooling if that suits the family- learning through exploration and self-initiated research. The important thing is that learning during a period of deschooling isn't forced- that children are allowed time to transition out of the performance mindset and discover the joy and reward that learning can be in itself.

Deschooling is important for the family unit, as well. In public school, a family spends very little time together, but homeschoolers spend most of their waking hours interacting with each other. This change in itself can cause a strain as dynamics change and family members realize that they really do not know each other as well as they thought they did.

The reality is that the decision to homeschool is a big one, and it is life-altering for everyone involved. It should be treated as such. When families move out of state, lose a loved one, or encounter some other drastic upheaval in their day-to-day lives, it is normal- and expected- that they will take some time to process and adjust to the changes. That is what deschooling is- stopping to take a breath during a period of perceived chaos. It is ok to take a break, and it is especially important if making the change in the middle of the school year.

Education is not a checklist to work through, and it should not have a timeline etched in stone. Education is a journey that a homeschool family takes together, and it means shared experiences and learning alongside each other. That means, that it is ok to slow down as necessary so that family members are able to be engaged in the learning process.

For families who are accustomed to the rigorous demands of public school, deschooling is a crucial step toward rediscovering a love for learning that comes so easily in most homeschool environments. Homeschooling should not look anything like public school- it is fundamentally different in that it usually focuses on the individual child's needs and interests, rather than the outline approved by the school board.

This does not mean that homeschool students do not learn critical skills like reading and writing. On the contrary, essential skills are often taught using resources that are of unique interest to the child. Many children want to learn how to read and do math, because they recognize that these abilities will enable them to do bigger things- things that they really want to do. Because learning is more organic, it is easier to identify the logical sequence of events and the basic skills as tools to whatever end the student is pursuing.

Deschooling enables students and their families to re-orient themselves to this different approach to learning, so it is easier to see the big picture of what is being pursued. It helps families to adjust to a new normal without becoming overwhelmed. Ultimately, it can help students and their families fall in love with learning again.

Homeschooling Multiple Students

As with so many other elements of the homeschool journey, learning to teach multiple students at once is a process that evolves over time. Since time is limited and the demand for attention is high, it is essential to find ways to maximize one's efficiency while teaching.

If children are close in age, many parents choose to teach subjects such as history and literature together, allowing the children to have a "classmate" for a time, so time can be devoted to one subject lesson instead of two. This can be done for any subject where children share a similar level of understanding. This is, perhaps, the simplest way to teach multiple students at once.

If teaching multiple students the same material is not feasible, additional planning may be required. It may be helpful to make a list of each child's school subjects, and mark the ones that require the most one-on-one help, so those subjects can be scheduled around each other. Subjects that one student is able to complete independently can be worked on while siblings that require assistance work with a parent.

Teaching style will vary a lot depending on the parent and the students, but flexibility and availability are essential. Sometimes, teaching multiples means sitting between them while they work on their respective subjects, and answering questions as they come up. Sometimes, it means skipping a subject with one if the other requires extra help. Some days, not everything will get done, and that is ok. The important thing is that children are able to learn at their own pace.

There are advantages to teaching multiple children, too. If one child is exceptionally good at a subject, they may enjoy helping to teach a younger sibling. Teaching is its own beneficial skill, and it has been said that a person who is able to teach their material truly understands it. Allowing children the opportunity to work together and help each other develops compassion, patience, communication, organization, and leadership skills. Allowing students to learn together teaches camaraderie, trust, communication, and interpersonal skills.

Parents tend to put a lot of pressure on themselves, thinking that they have to do everything on their own. However, it is ok to delegate, and often there are benefits to allowing children to figure things out together, or even to homeschooling alongside another family.

Some families teach multiple children by planning a couple of days a week with another family and splitting up the teaching responsibilities. This works well for families who have children the same ages, and one parent can teach one set of children while the other teaches the other. It is not usually a daily exercise, but it can help alleviate some of the stress of teaching alone while allowing for some social interactions for students and parents.

The important thing to remember while starting this process, especially for parents who are new to homeschooling, is that it is a skill that develops over time- for parents and students. It is ok to ease into homeschooling instead of jumping in all at once and overwhelming everyone involved. There is nothing wrong with starting slowly. After a period of deschooling it may be easier for children to begin with a couple of things at a time, or a few days a week, and increase once it is comfortable. If working part time with students, one could even alternate days for each student, so they can take turns having the individualized attention that they need.

Progress is progress, and as long as everyone is moving forward toward a common goal- however slowly- the family will succeed. Homeschooling is not a one-size-fits-all approach to learning. It is different for every family, and it can change yearly, weekly, or daily. Let it. Do not get hung up on the details, or discouraged by a bad day. Learning happens, even when we do not realize it is happening. Focus on the basics, and move on from there.

Resources:

Homeschool Planet- Online editable planner for schoolwork, activities, and chores with option for multiple user profiles (www.homeschoolplanet.com)

Homeschool.com- Free downloads, podcasts, parent resources, curriculum reviews (www.homeschool.com)

IXL- Creates customized lesson plans for students based on course work evaluated by actional analytics, giving parents real-time feedback on student progress and learning gaps, tailored to state requirements. Available for individual or multiple subjects. (www.ixl.com)

Life Unboxed- Encouragement, strategies, words of wisdom for homeschool parents who also work from home (www.lifeunboxed.blog)

Homeschooling with Littles

Homeschooling with littles is often seen as one of the more daunting enterprises, because young children are difficult to predict and often unwilling to cooperate with the requests of a parent, particularly if it means they do not get to be a part of what the older ones are doing. Young children like to be in the center of whatever happens to be going on at the time. It is how they learn, but it can also make structured learning for older siblings a challenge. Parents often take advantage of nap times for work that requires more parental involvement, but nap time is not always long enough to fit in all of the day's requirements.

One solution to this problem is to find a way to allow younger children to "participate" if they choose to- whether it is an extra copy of a worksheet for them to scribble on, sitting on your lap while reading, playing with a quiet toy in the vicinity, or some other activity that makes them feel included. As counterintuitive as it is for some parents, this is often a simple solution to the problem.

Children, and especially young children, learn through interaction, imitation, and observation, so the more time they are able to spend doing what the rest of the family is doing, the more naturally they will adapt to the same behaviors as they get older. Often times, young children will "participate" for a short while and then get bored and move on to something else on their own. That is perfectly fine, and a much more peaceful arrangement than trying to persuade them to entertain themselves from the beginning. Children who are allowed to listen in tend to learn from the lessons, too, so teaching younger children may be easier than teaching their older siblings, simply because they "absorb" a lot before their years of formal teaching have even begun.

In our house, we have a small playroom full of Montessori-type learning supplies- a keyboard, a buffet table full of art supplies, an organizer with blocks, cars, puzzles, and other toys that promote problem-solving and creative play. This room is adjacent to the living room, where most of our reading work is done. This has been a nice set up for us, because our children are able to wander back and forth between the living room and play room- the littles are within earshot of the lessons that are taking place, and they are able to go play on their own without feeling like they are "missing out" on something. Older and younger kids are able to see each other, and it makes for a very fluid learning environment. This is just one example of what a home learning environment can look like.

Another strategy that is very useful, is setting up activity stations around the kitchen table for children to rotate through. For example, one may have kinetic sand, one may have puzzles, one may have blocks, one may have coloring books. Each child chooses a station to start at and a timer is set for a pre-determined amount of time- ten or fifteen minutes, maybe more, depending on the age of the children and their attention span. When the timer goes off, the children leave the station they are at and move on to the next one. This is repeated until every child has had an opportunity to play at every station. If there are four stations and the timer is set for fifteen minutes per rotation, that can free up an hour to work with older kids on their lessons, or gives the parent a chance to breathe.

There are a number of benefits to activity stations. They keep messes contained, teach children in a very basic way about the passage of time, taking turns, cooperation with peers, and children are able to share their progress with their siblings in real time while also working independently. This strategy can be more effective than simply leaving children in a room to play, because there is a natural interest that develops from watching others enjoy something. Children get to anticipate their turn at an activity while simultaneously showing off their work to the others. Once children understand that they will get a turn doing all of the activities, there tends to be less quarrelling.

As with almost everything in homeschooling, the process is all about trying different possibilities to see what works best for your family and your unique teaching/ learning style. There is not one right or wrong way of doing things, but understanding how

children learn and trying to "work smarter not harder" by allowing

littles to participate as much as they can/want to can make the

process much easier for everyone.

Teaching the Dyslexic/Dysgraphic Child

Some children do not process information the way their peers do, and this can cause additional doubts as parents question their ability to teach the child. For this chapter, I interviewed Michele Moore- a homeschool mom who also mentors others in teaching children with unique learning styles. Her insight was very helpful and encouraging, and she made the prospect of teaching one of these special learners seem very manageable.

Michele explained that dyslexic children see words differently. They may see letters reversed or words backwards, and for some it looks like letters are falling off the page. Students with dyslexia tend to struggle with reading and spelling. She said the secret to teaching them is to figure out what makes sense to them and teach them that way, because the end goal is to help them learn to read and write and function independently in society. If one can accomplish that, it does not matter how it is done. Some tools that she recommends trying include books with bigger/different font, paper or a notecard to hold under a line to "keep the letters from falling," and rewriting work pages to create more space between problems.

Michele went on to explain, "if a child is in a wheelchair, you make accommodations- you build a ramp, install elevators, etc- whatever the child needs so they can participate in day-to-day activities. Teaching children is the same way- if a child learns a specific way, it is our job, as parents and adults, to accommodate the needs of the child to help them succeed. They should not have to make accommodations for us."

According to Sutton and Fields, there are ten helpful strategies for teaching students with dyslexia/dysgraphia. First, is explicit, direct instruction in phonological and phonemic skills; children with dyslexia benefit from systematic, direct, and explicit phonics instruction that is also multi-sensory (including visual, audio, and kinesthetic learning mechanisms). Second is the use of "dyslexic-friendly" fonts, such as Comic Sans, Century Gothic,

Times New Roman, and Dyslexie. They also recommend personalized, time-driven (not task-driven) homework that is broken up into smaller pieces as necessary; color coding and labelling that is clear and consistent; and space, lighting, and noise-control to aid with concentration. They also recommend shorter tasks, flexible deadlines, and additional time allotted for reading assignments and tests. Reduced stress in the environment, experienced teacher mentors, Assistive Technology (AT), and building resilience and self-esteem are also especially beneficial for students with dyslexia (Shields, 2016).

We have gotten used to an education system that says learning is supposed to be done a certain way. There is one standard, one method, and then we are surprised when children who do not fit the mold get lost in the shuffle. It simply should not be that way. Differences in learning style should be acknowledged- and celebrated- the way so many other differences are celebrated. Many of the great minds throughout history were great simply because they had a unique way of viewing the world, and that translated into art, music, scientific discoveries, and inventions that were meaningful to others.

It is important to recognize that everyone, including children, has strengths and weaknesses. Some are more obvious than others, but every individual is born with a combination of both, and children with dyslexia/dysgraphia are no different. According to a study by Julie Sutton and Marion Shields, "Students with dyslexia all exhibit a shared commonality of core indicators that include difficulty with phonological processing in decoding (reading) and encoding (spelling) activities (IDA, 2015) simultaneously exhibiting strengths in areas such as creative thinking, reasoning, problem solving, conceptual abilities, comprehending, 3-D construction, seeing the big picture (Shaywitz, 2005) and can also display giftedness in areas that don't require strong literacy skills (Karten, 2015)" (Shields, 2016).

While it is important for children to learn how to read and write, it is also beneficial to highlight the strengths they have in other areas, instead of focusing on their struggles. By giving them opportunities to, a parent can not only help them to feel confident in the skills they do possess, but can also help them to feel more like a person whose brain thinks differently, rather than someone whose brain does not work correctly. That small shift in focus can have a huge impact on a child's self-confidence and motivation.

Parents need to know that it is ok to do things differently. That it is better for everyone if they teach the child instead of teaching the system. More than education, it is an opportunity for building trust and bonding, as parent and child get to know and understand each other better and pursue a common goal in a way that works for everyone.

Children should not feel like they are "lesser" because their minds work differently, but should be able to communicate their needs and expect that, to the best of our abilities, we will help them achieve their goals in the best possible way. This camaraderie is essential to build the child's confidence and enthusiasm toward learning- knowing that they have an ally who will come alongside and help them, and that the reason they struggle may have less to do with them and more to do with the method of instruction. Suddenly, instead of the child being the problem, they get to be a part of figuring out the solution.

Resources for Parents of Students with Dyslexia

Books:

The Dyslexic Advantage by Brock and Fernette Eide

The Dyslexia Empowerment Plan: A Blueprint for Renewing Your Child's Confidence and Love of Learning by Ben Foss

The Gift of Dyslexia by Ronald D. Davis (The Davis Method)

Overcoming Dyslexia by Sally Shaywitz M.D.

Seeing What Others Cannot See: The Hidden Advantages of Visual Thinkers and Differently Wired Brains by Thomas G. West

Teacher Mentors:

My Homeschool Hub (www.myhomeschoolhub.com)

Teaching the Child with Attention Deficit Hyperactive Disorder (ADHD)

It has become increasingly more common to hear about children with Attention Deficit Hyperactive Disorder (ADHD). An estimated eight percent of students are diagnosed with ADHD during the course of their school career, and it is often first identified as an inability to focus, follow instruction, or sit still (American Psychiatric Association, 2022).

There are three main types of ADHD- inattentive type, hyperactive/impulsive, and combined type. Inattentive types tend to lose focus easily, they are disorganized, and have difficulty following through with tasks that require extensive thought or time. Hyperactive/Impulsive types have difficulty sitting still, talk a lot, and can tend to take over conversations/activities or act in ways that seem over-the-top for the situation. Combined type consists of some blend of the two (American Psychiatric

Association, 2022).

Children with ADHD tend to have more difficulty in a

classroom setting because of the number of potential distractions in

the room and the limited movement allowed. Some parents choose

to medicate their child to calm them down and enable them to

participate better in a classroom environment.

Peg Dawson EdD and Richard Guare PhD write, "There is

an emerging consensus among researchers that ADHD is

fundamentally a disorder of executive skills. Russell Barkley, for

example, sees the disorder as one of reduced ability to self-

regulate. While a number of executive skills can be affected,

response inhibition is key among these and impacts development

of the other executive skills… Chief among these are response

inhibition, sustained attention, working memory, time

management, task initiation, and goal-directed persistence" (PhD,

2009).

They also say, "…The frontal lobes, and therefore executive skills, will require 18-20 years, or even longer, to develop fully. Given these factors, children cannot rely solely on their own frontal lobes to regulate behavior. What's the solution? We lend them our frontal lobes. Although we may not think of it in these terms, parenting is, among other things, a process of providing executive skills support and coaching for our children" (PhD, 2009).

Homeschooling is beneficial for the child with ADHD for a number of reasons. Besides having the constant and consistent "executive skills support" described above, teaching at home provides more flexibility to accommodate what makes the child comfortable.

Classroom protocol for teaching children with ADHD includes a very strict and predictable environment, where everything is structured and there is limited distraction. While good for short periods of intense focus, it is a very uncomfortable environment to try to work in for eight hours every day, even for adults. In fact, it may be doing these children a great disservice, as it disregards some of their most notable strengths.

Mitch Fodstad highlights seven key traits of the ADHD child that are highly unique and worth celebrating. According to Fodstad, children with ADHD have a unique perspective on the world. They are great out-of-the-box thinkers. They are highly curious, creative, and have the ability to "hyperfocus" on things that are of interest to them. Children with ADHD are more willing to take risks as they are naturally more impulsive, and they have high energy for things that are of interest to them (Fodstad, 2018). In short, they are highly motivated by subjects that are stimulating to them, and are able to problem solve in ways that the average person cannot. They can be creators, scientists, inventors, and entrepreneurs. Rather than fight against their natural curiosity and drive, it is advantageous to take advantage of their strengths and allow them to explore the things that motivate them.

When a child is at home, they can have the freedom to listen to schoolwork sitting upside down, or while playing with Legos if they choose to. They are able to get up and move as needed, or change the order of their coursework to add some variety to the day. As a homeschool teacher, a parent also has the freedom to give the curious child some control over their learning, and even use it as an incentive. A child with ADHD may find bookwork mundane, but may have an easier time completing it if they are able to finish their day with a subject that they want to do- a documentary, an educational You Tube video- something else that they are intensely interested in. For the ADHD child, the promise of a chance to learn what they want to learn can be highly motivating and may make it easier for them to focus on the schoolwork that precedes it in order to get to the subject matter they really want to learn.

The strength of homeschooling is a very individualized approach to education, and a chance to unleash a child's full potential by letting them explore the things that they are passionate about. Children with full, eight-hour school days and copious amounts of homework hardly have time for anything else, let alone pursuing additional interests, but homeschool children with more free time and more control of their schedules are able to get a jump start on figuring out what they want to choose as a career field.

Every person- every child- is unique and has their own strengths to contribute to society. Their education should be just as individualized as they are. Children should be allowed to pursue their own interests, and in doing so learn to be self-motivated, independent workers with the ability to problem solve and the confidence to pave their own way in the world.

College Admissions for Homeschoolers

One of the most common concerns that new homeschoolers express is the issue of college enrollment, and wanting to make sure that their children will have the resources they need to be competitive when trying to get into their college of choice. It is daunting to think that a child's education rests solely on the shoulders of their parents, and since the parents are not trained "educators," maybe something will be missed. Parents do not need to have a degree in education in order to teach a child to read and write, and if there is a subject that the parent is less knowledgeable in, it is easy enough to recruit help teaching the subject in question. Homeschooling is less about knowing all of the answers, and more about finding resources to meet a child's specific needs.

It is good for parents to be aware that, more and more, colleges are seeking out homeschooled students to recruit, because they tend to be more respectful and more engaged at school, as well as more self-motivated (Weller, 2015). This awareness may help parents feel less overwhelmed, knowing that they only need to teach their children well. Parents do not need to go above and beyond to create a stellar resume for their children (though many parents naturally do), because the case has already been made for homeschool students. They have a reputation of excellence, simply for the fact that they statistically perform better in basic subjects, and they are better at adapting to various social situations. They are an asset to whatever college or workplace they choose.

This being the case, the main expectation on parents is to compile a high school transcript for the student that shows they are a good candidate for the degree they want to pursue. This does not mean making up course work that does not exist, but making space to showcase the student's interest and previous exposure to whatever subject material may set them apart from their peers. Here, too, homeschool parents have more flexibility in defining coursework, or including extracurricular activities that will set their child apart during the application process.

As students advance into high school, homeschoolers often choose to substitute community college courses for similar homeschool classes. Much like the dual-credit system many schools use to help students transition into college, community college classes for homeschoolers help to bridge whatever gap there may be, and provide homeschoolers with a GPA that colleges can look at, whereas a lot of homeschoolers graduate without a formal GPA rating. Community college classes for homeschoolers can help to reassure any skeptic that the homeschool student is well prepared for the challenges of college. College applications can be much like job resumes. They can include past work, highlight volunteer work, hobbies, classes, or other relevant experiences.

Individual requirements vary by state (Homeschool Legal Defense Association, 2021), so it is important to be mindful of what those are and take them into consideration during the education process and when assembling a final transcript for the student. Most states expect some form of record keeping or portfolio to prove that learning is happening, and many also require periodic standardized testing. These things can be incorporated into college applications, and major projects that highlight the student's skills are especially beneficial.

Many schools also offer scholarships for homeschool students who demonstrate a lot of potential, as do many organizations that homeschool students may choose to be a part of. The secret to an easy college application process is to plan ahead and look for opportunities well in advance, so it is easier to prepare ahead of time for them.

Homeschool parents may worry about their students potentially being at a disadvantage during the college application process, but the reality is that homeschoolers are very competitive when it comes to college admissions. Some colleges take GPA into consideration, many are much more interested in SAT/ACT scores, special projects, and extracurricular involvement. Because of this, and because of the reputation that homeschool students have developed over time amongst institutions, homeschool students are very competitive when applying for college.

Resources:

https://homeeducator.com/scholarships/ - scholarships, grants, internships, and college entrance information for homeschoolers

https://fearlesshomeschoolers.com/blog/scholarships-for-homeschoolers - guide to scholarships and financial aid for homeschool students

https://www.listsofscholarships.com/homeschool-scholarships/ - Searchable list of scholarships that is periodically being updated

https://hslda.org/community/grants-for-homeschooling - grants for homeschoolers *https://www.thehomeschoolmom.com/high-school-beyond/high-school-homeschool-transcript/* - free homeschool transcript template

Extending Grace

Homeschooling is hard. Parenting is hard. Many parents find the two to be the hardest- and most rewarding- things they ever do. There are some important things to remember when beginning your homeschooling journey.

First, homeschooling is a marathon, not a sprint. This means that there is time to figure it out as you go, and not everything has to be taught in a day. In fact, there is value to giving children time to process, and even sleep on, information before visiting it again or moving on. Quite often, children may struggle with something the first day, but will understand it better the second day after they've had time to organize their thoughts in their sleep. (The human brain does a lot of information processing during sleep.) It is ok to introduce information, move on to something else, and revisit the first concept the following day (or week or month). It is ok, and often less overwhelming, to touch a subject multiple times, so that it seeps in little by little, each time becoming a little less foreign.

It is also important to remember that homeschooling is a journey, and it will look a little bit different for every single person- and family- who tries it. This means that it is ok if your homeschool curriculum is not the same as anyone else's- the important thing is that you figure out what works for your family, and it is ok if you do not get it right the first time. Try something. If it does not work the way you hoped it would then try something else. Inventors, scientists, and creators do it all the time, and as a parent to a young mind who is only beginning to discover its potential, you have the freedom to do the same.

If a child struggles in a particular area, it does not mean that you are failing as a teacher, it simply means that you have not found the best way to teach that child, or that they are not ready to learn it yet. Take a break, and try something else. If you believe they can accomplish the goal, they will, too.

Remember that life happens, and it is ok to allow for that, too. Properly handling unforeseen circumstances as they arise will mean that more focused attention can be given to studies at the proper time, too. Each state has its boxes to check to complete the "school year," but school is more about an end goal than about filling out a checklist. Quality is more important than quantity, and a child who is engaged and motivated is much easier to teach than one who has given up and decided that it is too hard.

Ultimately, I hope readers understand that it is ok to extend grace- to oneself and to others. It is ok to have bad days, it is ok to take breaks, and it is ok for children to come back to something that is a struggle for them. Many people are afraid of making a mistake and so they fail to even try. But mistakes are always a part of the learning process. If you look at it as an opportunity to get to know your child better- as a science experiment to see what works and what does not- maybe there will be less of an inclination to feel like a failure.

The biggest disservice you can do to your child when it comes to schooling, is not taking the initiative to try something that you think will help them because you are afraid you may not do it well enough. If you learn together and develop trust and communication- if you extend each other grace- then even struggles can be a positive experience as you try to work through the challenges together. Challenges are a natural part of life. The choice you make is not whether or not they exist, but the nature of the challenges and whether or not you are willing to walk through them with your child.

It can be overwhelming to feel like it is up to you to make sure your child knows everything they need. You do not have to do it alone. It may take some time to find your village, but there are a lot of resources available. The Homeschool Legal Defense Association (HSLDA) has a search tool to help build your local network; many social media platforms have local homeschooling groups that enable parents to connect with each other; quick searches on the internet will show local homeschool coops your family can join. The hardest part is getting started, but once you take the initial step it will not take long to become integrated into your local homeschool community, and you will likely be surprised by how big and vibrant it is.

Homeschool communities are a special thing, because other homeschool families intimately know the challenges and rewards that come with this special calling. Because of this, they are eager to help each other out, and work to try and support each other in their efforts. Homeschool parents are quick to acknowledge their own weaknesses and the prudent ones find ways to compensate, either in a coop setting or by sharing homeschool days with parents who have other strengths. By supporting each other, homeschool parents are able to offer their children a much more robust school experience, and the opportunity to seek out their own unique strengths.

Parents have long been discouraged from teaching their kids, because they are told that they are not qualified, and do not know as much about teaching children as those who have gone to school and have completed special training. It is hard to get out of the mindset that we are only second best and may end up traumatizing our kids in some way. And yet, studies show that homeschool students score significantly higher on standardized testing, SAT/ACT, they are better prepared for the "real world" after school, and they are more socially mature, regardless of their parents' qualifications to teach (Brian D. Ray, 2021). The thing that children need most to succeed are parents who are actively engaged and invested in their lives, and if parents and students work together toward a common goal, the relationships built will extend far beyond school age.

Appendix

Testimonies and words of wisdom from seasoned homeschoolers, for those who are just beginning their own homeschool journeys.

"I've always known I wanted to homeschool. The seeds were planted for this during my own government school education. I knew the books weren't telling the truth about some things. I had first-hand experience. Thank goodness my husband was on board!

We had no framework for educating at home other than to try and replicate the typical government school classroom, and adding in our Christian faith. Home education is a paradigm shift and requires kicking down the walls of our understanding of what education really is and having the confidence knowing that we CAN educate our children. No college education or training is necessary—only a desire to do right by our kids.

On our journey we discovered the classical model of education, which was another paradigm shift. At the beginning it was a free fall of sorts—trusting the process to yield good fruit. As my children are all now teens, the oldest about to graduate, the fruits are on full display. Instead of teaching them WHAT to think, we've taught them HOW to think. We've imparted logic, both formal and informal. We've taught them how to learn, as learning never ceases. We've taught them confidence as they learn to share what they've learned and how to impart their knowledge to others. Their foundations are built on rock in the shifting sands of society.

Though the reasons for choosing home education were varied to begin with, our reasons for continuing have morphed and are vaster than they once were. We have had the opportunity to monitor the character development of our kids, pour Jesus into them, develop strong bonds with them and they with each other, provide flexibility and teach them how to do life in practical ways that we might have missed had they been away all day. Every year we discover new reasons to homeschool. This is a decision I have never regretted one single day.   –Vara B.

It was July 2020 as our family was vacationing in Ft. Myers Beach during the height of COVID-19. Schools in KY were debating what to do with the 2020-2021 School Year. At the time my oldest was a rising senior and my youngest was a rising freshman. Instead of vacationing, I was researching homeschooling.

My biggest fear was that the schools were not prepared for a dramatic shift to online teaching. I didn't want the kids GPAs to be affected by this. I read what the plans were for their school district, looked at other school districts in the area, considered established online public schools that we didn't have access to.

We decided that our oldest could take dual credit college classes and enrolled him in the electrical program at our community college. We paid 1/3 of the tuition rate and he qualified for 2 scholarships that paid his tuition for 2 classes at 100%. We chose to homeschool our freshman and had her take the college entrance exam for math. She tested into college algebra, but our local community college refused to take her because she wasn't a junior. We found another KY community college that would.

My son completed his first year of college as a homeschooled senior. Our daughter took college algebra and earned a 98.5% in that class. She missed the social interaction, and we re-enrolled her in our local school district to complete her freshman year. Her sophomore year, the high school allowed her to continue taking college coursework. In the end, I feel like it was very helpful in comparison to their classmates who seem to have fallen behind educationally since the COVID pandemic.

– Destiny C.

"I was raised as a homeschooler and as much as I loved being homeschooled when I had children I knew I didn't want to homeschool. Teaching is not a natural talent, and my patience level isn't the highest! I labeled myself unable to teach my own children in my mind.

Then covid happened. With decisions being made and with the solutions to the problems at hand being worse than the problem, I knew I had to make a change. I had a daughter going into 2nd grade, a son going into kindergarten, and a toddler. God convicted me - telling me, 'You may not want to, but you can, and I will help you!'

So 2020 was the beginning of my homeschool journey. It was hard to get going and it is still hard, but it's worth it. It has taken many start overs and reality checks, but I know this is what I need to be doing. We have had a period of "unschooling." Meaning, we were once in a school setting and now we are having to learn that doing school at home does not have to look like school in building with a set schedule and the same curriculum for all. All three of my children learn differently. Grace needs to be given to ourselves and our children.

Homeschooling is not just learning from books, it's character building, teaching life skills, teaching them how to communicate their own thoughts, and not just what we think they should say. I could go on, but if I had to label what homeschooling really is for us it is better labeled as life development. Homeschooling is not just the time that we sit together and do workbooks - it's a lifestyle. I am thankful that God used 2020 to open my eyes to the ability that I have in myself through Him to teach my three children at home while also working with my husband in our own business.

Our children are getting to view the world in a completely different way. They are able to retain much of their innocence while also being able to grasp life skills that are rarely taught. I was never against homeschooling even though I didn't want to do it, but now that I am doing it myself I am not sure you will find a stronger advocate. It will not only change your children – it will change you!"

–Ashton C.

"To provide some background about myself, I am a mom of 4 sons, ages 15, 14, 12, and 9. I am a professional educator myself and have been teaching for a total of 12 years. I taught at a small private (non-Christian) school for 3 years before having my first son. I was then a stay-at-home mom for 8 years. My youngest son was about 4 months old when my husband and I decided it was time for me to go back to teaching.

At that time, we were at a crossroads with his small business, and he was going to be the one to stay home with the kids and do a variety of jobs from home or jobs with a more flexible schedule that did not require him to work a regular 9 to 5, Monday through Friday job. At that time, when I returned to teaching, I got my credential to teach students with disabilities. For the past 8 years, I have been an educator in the public school system in Colorado and work with students with disabilities, which I absolutely love.

My husband and I have experience and a unique perspective from having our children in all 3 school settings: the public school system, homeschool, and private Christian school. My husband is currently a Pastor and our perspective and convictions about education have changed over the last 15 years. We both grew up being educated by the public school system. Our sons currently attend a local private Christian school. They are thriving and it has been an answer to our prayers and a great blessing.

We started our sons in the public school system because we did not have all of the convictions we do now around education. In addition to that, at the time, the public school system was not as strict towards Christians, and was not pushing the LGBTQ agenda as vigorously as it is now. Currently, the federal government is pushing an agenda within the school systems and requiring schools to teach sex education and gender theory at an early age. Schools are now required to have bathrooms for students who identify as the opposite sex and are not allowed to counsel a child who is struggling with gender identity.

With all those changes that recently came down the pipeline over the last few years, my husband and I decided it was time to pull our children from public education. The public school system is an anti-God, anti-Biblical environment. There are wonderful Christians who work in the public school system, but they are strictly prohibited from sharing their faith and preaching the gospel or saying anything about God. Children spend a lot of time at school, and we did not want our children subjected to an unbiblical, secular perspective, and ideologies and influences primarily from non-Christians. Since private Christian education can be quite costly, we figured that our first initial solution to this change in convictions would be to homeschool our children.

Jumping into the homeschool realm was quite a culture shock, to say the least. We quickly found it was very difficult to do a good job with all 4 of our children in all the different academic areas that they needed to be educated in. We felt that there was not enough time in the day to be able to meet the needs of each child academically. My husband and I were spending hours during the week attempting to re-teach ourselves material that our older kids were learning, in order to teach them effectively. However, the biggest advantage and blessing to homeschooling was the ability to disciple our children and develop godly character in them. That is the element that I most value about home education. The ability to disciple your child and really work with them on addressing and weeding out bad character issues individually that they each struggle with.

Since we were going to have one child in high school, two children in middle school, and one child in elementary school, we decided to pursue private Christian education at a brick-and-mortar school. We felt that professional teachers with a biblical perspective, who have the freedom to share their Christian values with our children, would be the best setting for this season of life we are in. Our children have been attending a local Christian school and we have been very blessed with them being in this setting. All of the teachers and administrators are professing Christians and often my children come home excited about what they are learning about the Bible.

For our family, a private Christian school is currently the best fit and we have found the most satisfaction and desired results with them being in this setting. No education system is perfect, and parents must approach the subject with diligent prayer and consideration to decide for themselves what is the best choice for their family. Parents have an obligation before the Lord to educate their children in a Biblical, God glorifying environment. One must choose very carefully and wisely whom they are sending their child to be discipled by. Your children will be discipled by someone; who do you want that to be?" – Katie U.

"What a fun opportunity to think about the work that the Lord Jesus Christ has done in our lives through focus on Him along with homeschooling our nine children! We have absolutely loved homeschooling all nine of our children from elementary school through high school. Statistics say we get four extra years' worth of time with our children if we homeschool them.

My husband and I are not as high achievers academically as people we know. I would say we do academics because we should.

The most important school subjects are language arts and math. These should be a priority and studied daily. Language arts is needed to function in life, and a math test is the only non-subjective test. My husband tutors the children in higher math.

Five of our nine children are adults. They all started college at our local community college. The ones with Bachelors degrees graduated from our local university. It isn't difficult to get into a community college then transfer to a university. We find it hard to believe that any university would turn a student away when they are making such exorbitant amounts of money off of each student. Anyway, all were able to pass the community college Accuplacer test within the first two tries.

Here are a few details about our adult children:

1. 33 year old- Bachelors degree in Nursing, Nightingale Award nominee, CEN (Certified Emergency Nurse), trained as a paramedic, charge nurse and pediatric ER nurse

2. 31 year old- Bachelors in history, midwife student 6 years, attended 115 births, insurance collections for a large hospital conglomeration, quality assurance and business analytics, business systems analyst

3. 29 year old- Bachelors in computer science, worked for a defense corporation 12 years, now works for himself in signal processing developing/engineering

4. 27 year old- certified paramedic, moved to Indiana where paramedics are state funded and have high wages, plans to go back to college this fall

5. 22 year old- successfully runs our family metal finishing business- a great fit for his personality and abilities.

We encouraged the route of starting at a community college because of our desire for them to have no debt. Some achieved their college goals without debt and without our financial help. Our children have excelled in their respective fields, and some have been able to do things that most people only dream of, like pay cash for a new home.

Ways our children think homeschooling benefited them:

- Homeschooling helped me learn how to work and communicate with a wider range of people, and to be confident that it is fine to be different.

- Homeschooling helped me to learn that being outside of the box is alright.

- By being homeschooled, I spent more time around adults than only people my age. I think I can relate to people of all ages better and probably am more mature because of it.

- It made me feel responsible for my own education, which has made it easier for me to keep learning.

- I got better than my peers in my interests because I was able to pursue my interests." – Bobbie H.

"When my family was trying to decide what route we should take for our child's education, we started looking at schools that were close by. We wanted a place that we could trust to love our son and take the time to educate him well. Our daily prayers were crafted after this thought. I imagined a school that was happy, full of life, entertaining, but also full of opportunities to expand and help my son grow into the ideal student. After all, he is my son and we wanted to provide him with the very best!

When my son was four, my husband and I chose what we thought was the perfect education path. Our number one pick was a private school that had excellent reviews and one that, after touring a few schools, was the one we thought would offer the most possibilities for excellence. The teachers were amazing, the curriculum demanding but appropriate, including learning how to play violin and write in cursive. On top of this, the school was well gated and guarded, a top priority we were unwilling to budge on.

Then we moved, and our best laid plans fell through. My husband suggested that we homeschool for that year, but I felt completely inadequate, and feared my son would fall behind. However, my desire for him to learn and grow without delay was stronger than my fear of being his teacher.

We got to work looking for programs, and aids to help us to instruct our son. Since that day, our family has grown to love homeschooling. So much so, that we never have turned back or regretted this path. Our personal endeavors to find him the best education we could find began simply with our love for him.

We have chosen our own schedule, curriculum, activities, mentors, and scholars to teach, guide, and help our son. And this ability to personalize his education has helped him to thrive.

One of the greatest aspects of instructing our son has been that we have spent a great deal of time with him over the years. The number one objection that I hear from parents is that they would not want to spend all day with their children, that they would go insane. Yes, we do need to rejuvenate to be the best version of ourselves, but one thing that we will never regret is our time with our son. We have learned together, and grown in many, many ways. Trusting ourselves through the grace of our Heavenly Father, we have gained knowledge continually from those on the journey before us.

Our compass for learning has been turned to classic literature, history, and other scholars that understand what we have not known or been able to teach. We also spend a great deal of time at the library, where information and searching for knowledge is often easily available.

Homeschooling is the most wonderful opportunity to meet lots of people, explore the community with your child, engage with all age groups, and ensure the best for your children. There is no better approach to helping your child become their own scholar." – Leah B.

"My name is Heather Smith, and I celebrated my 27th wedding anniversary last June (to the same man)! We have nine children ranging in age from twenty-four to nine. In fact, my bookends have the exact same birthday, just fifteen years apart. I have graduated all my 'bigs,' (oldest three), and one of my 'middles.' This is the second year that I have five in school. This is my nineteenth year of homeschooling.

The most important thing that I want to do is encourage you that YOU. CAN. DO. THIS! YOU CAN! Just like you TAUGHT your kidlets to walk, taught them to talk and pronounce words correctly, you taught them to feed themselves, you taught them to tie their shoes, you taught them to use the potty chair and to sleep in their big boy or big girl bed, how to interact with people at the store or the doctor's office or how to sit still in church, to look both ways to cross the street, not run in the parking lot, etc. You've already taught them so much!

You and I are alike- we're parents! Whether we have one or any other number of kids, we are alike. We all want what is best for our kids and to help them thrive.

WHY do you want to do this? I asked myself and realized that I had answered it forty-some-odd years ago when I KNEW that I wanted a lot of kids and I told my mom, 'I wanna have twelve kids when I grow up!' to which she ever so gently reached over, patted my arm, and told me, 'Why don't you have one first.'

See, for me, I didn't want to *have* them to just check off a list, I wanted to *be there* to experience life with them. That was *my* answer. Whatever *your* reason, there's no wrong one. They are *your* children, and you have the right to educate them in the manner you think best suits them, because every child is different.

WHAT does it look like? It looks like the weekend, reading, writing, and arithmetic, electives (being able to deep dive into learning about things they're interested in), home economics (learning how to properly clean, change a tire, price shop for necessary items, cook, grocery shop…), character building, music, and sports. You get to experience all of life together.

WHAT will you need? You're going to need Jesus. I realize that religious freedom may not be on some peoples' radar, some people don't believe in God or feel that those who do are weak, etc. However, what I'm trying to convey to you is that in your own strength you can only do so much. That goes for each one of us. But, when you've come to the end of your rope and it's only 10am you're going to need the strength from another source greater than yourself.

The Bible says in Philippians 4:13 that "I can do ALL things (which includes homeschooling my kids, living peaceably with my neighbor, loving my spouse when he or she is being not-so-nice, and allowing Him to teach and train me and cause me to grow in Him) through Him who gives me strength."

We need His strength because we're going to see the junk in *us* in such a magnified way because we are staring it in the face each and every day with our kiddos. It's truly amazing how those little things that your kids do can make you insane… if you allow them to. Or, you always wonder why your child has to be practically under your feet- they've missed being with you. They may not know how to say it, but it's true none the less. Pull them up in your lap and read history, the Bible, literature or poetry books together… that may not be your cup of tea, but you don't have to do it all day long. Just make a point to give them special, focused time with mom or dad. Homeschooling is a challenge- it's mentally and emotionally draining. So we need to be in prayer.

Give yourself and your children grace. It takes time to learn how to teach your children, so give yourself, and them, time to learn. Let them see you try, and fail, and try again as you figure it out. It will give them courage to try to conquer their own mountains. Toss out expectations- don't compare yourself or your kids to anyone else. It will kill your joy. Your family is unique and special, and homeschooling will look different for your family than for others, and that's a *good* thing!

You need to have an open heart. With a truly open heart you will be able to see your kids for the gift that they are from God. He has given us children to steward and raise for what He has planned for their lives. What a responsibility! We need to learn to love our children right where they are, not where we want them to be or where we think they should be. Growing takes time, and transitioning to homeschool takes time for everyone, and everyone differently. That's ok! Remind one another that 'We're all new to this.'

Wherever you're at, whatever your family situation, you can make it happen. There isn't a magic bullet list, just a goal. And, with His help, you're going to do great!" – Heather S.

"So, I've been giving a lot of thought to why I homeschool my son, and I could probably write five pages worth, but the main reason is I don't want him to be neglected if he's struggling in certain areas. Homeschooling allows for extra time or care in an area that is harder for him, but homeschooling also allows him to move on in areas he loves. I want him to have confidence and not be made fun of for struggling by students or teachers (which is something I experienced in school and have heard has only gotten worse). It's also really fun to see his face light up when he finally gets something! I could go on, but I think that might be the simplest answer." – Brandy J.

My husband and I both have backgrounds in education, so it makes sense that we want to use that knowledge and training to teach our children. But beyond that, we want to build a God-centered and God-honoring curriculum where we have the final say on what and how our children learn- not from someone else's idea of what is best for kids that don't know.

State-accredited teachers are often hamstrung by discipline problems and required to present anti-Christian doctrine in their classrooms. We don't want this for our kids. By homeschooling, we can avoid issues like students getting bullied because they enjoy learning or aren't keeping up with the latest fashions and electronic gadgets, not to mention today's safety concerns in public schools.

We can provide stability through multiple military moves. We can spend more time with our children, getting to know them and shaping their characters. Our oldest will start kindergarten this fall, and we are excited to go on this journey with him. –Noelle R.

Index

Bibliography

Allen, J. (2016, April 27). *A Majority of U.S. 12th Graders Lack Proficiency*. Retrieved from Center for Education Reform: https://edreform.com/2016/04/a-majority-of-u-s-12th-graders-lack-proficiency/

Allison Metsch, M. (2019, August 9). *All Children Develop at Their Own Pace- Even an Educator's Child*. Retrieved from Children's Services Council of Broward County: https://www.cscbroward.org/news/all-children-develop-their-own-pace-even-educators-child

American Psychiatric Association. (2022, June). *What is ADHD?* Retrieved from www.psychiatry.org: https://www.psychiatry.org/patients-families/adhd/what-is-adhd

Angela Passarelli, D. K. (2011). *The Oxford Handbook of Lifelong Learning.* Oxford: Oxford University Press.

Blank, A. (2018, July 24). *Forbes Women*. Retrieved from www.forbes.com: https://www.forbes.com/sites/averyblank/2018/07/24/5-ways-to-become-an-independent-thinker-and-show-your-leadership/?sh=10e4020b24a1

Brian D Ray, P. (2000, April 10). *Academic Intrinsic Motivation in Homeschool Children.* Retrieved from

National Home Education Research Institute:
https://www.nheri.org/home-school-researcher-
academic-intrinsic-motivation-in-homeschooled-
children/

Brian D. Ray, P. (2021, July 1). *Research Facts on
Homeschooling*. Retrieved from National Home
Education Research Institute:
https://www.nheri.org/research-facts-on-
homeschooling/

Briggs, S. (2014, July 5). *InformED*. Retrieved from Open
Colleges:
https://www.opencolleges.edu.au/informed/feature
s/self-efficacy-and-learning/

Bruce W. Tuckman, T. L. (1992). Self-Believers are Self-
Motivated; Self-Doubters are Not. *Personality and
Individual Differences*, 425-428.

Butler, P. (2016, September 20). *No grammar schools, lots of
play: the secrets of Europe's top education system*.
Retrieved from The Guardian:
https://www.theguardian.com/education/2016/sep
/20/grammar-schools-play-europe-top-education-
system-finland-daycare

Butler, P. (2016, September 20). *No GrammarSchools, Lots of
Play: the Secrets of Europe's Top EducationSystem*.

Retrieved from The Guardian:
https://www.theguardian.com/education/2016/sep
/20/grammar-schools-play-europe-top-education-
system-finland-daycare

Carl Gabbard, L. R. (2015). *Early Childhood News.* Retrieved
from Games and Physical Play LS2015:
http://expgamesls2015.krystinamadej.com/wp-
content/uploads/2015/04/GabbardRodriguesArticle
.pdf

Cathy Duffy. (2021, March 31). *Classical Approach.* Retrieved
from Cathy Duffy Reviews:
https://cathyduffyreviews.com/glossary-of-
homeschool-terms/c-d/classical-approach

Cheryl Flink, A. K. (1990). Controlling Teaching Strategies:
Undermining Children's Self-Determination and
Performance. *Journal of Personality and Social
Psychology*, 916-924.

Claire E. Cameron, L. L. (2012). Fine Motor Skills and
Executive Function Both Contribute to Kindergarten
Achievement. *Society for Research in Childhood
Development*, 1229-1244.

Connections Academy. (2021, November 3).
*UNDERSTANDING MULTIPLE INTELLIGENCES AND
LEARNING STYLES.* Retrieved from Connections

Academy:
https://www.connectionsacademy.com/support/res
ources/article/learning-styles-multiple-
intelligences/

Evan L Ardiel, K. H. (2010). The importance of touch in
development. *Pediatrics and Child Health*.

Fields-Smith, C. (2020). *Exploring Single Black Mothers'
Resistance Through Homeschooling.* London: Palgrave
MacMillan.

Fodstad, M. (2018, October 13). *7 Traits of the ADHD Mind
that Promote Success*. Retrieved from
www.medium.com:
https://medium.com/@mitchfodstad/7-attributes-
of-the-adhd-mind-that-promote-success-
8845bb6a4a31#:~:text=Curiosity,unrelenting%20cu
riosity%20comes%20in%20handy.

Homeschool Legal Defense Association. (2021, August 21).
Retrieved from Homeschool Legal Defense
Association: https://hslda.org/

Kamenetz, A. (2016, April 27). *Most High School Seniors
Aren't College Or Career Ready, Says 'Nation's Report
Card'*. Retrieved from npr.org:
https://www.npr.org/sections/ed/2016/04/27/475

628214/most-high-school-seniors-arent-college-or-career-ready-says-nations-report-card

Laurio, L. N. (2004). *CM's 20 Principles*. Retrieved from Ambleside Online: https://www.amblesideonline.org/CM/20Principles.html

Leal, F. (2015, July 30). *Survey: Most high school students feel unprepared for college, careers*. Retrieved from EdSource: https://edsource.org/2015/survey-most-high-school-students-feel-unprepared-for-college-careers/83752

Marano, H. E. (2007, April 29). *Daycare: Raising Baby*. Retrieved from Psychology Today: https://www.psychologytoday.com/us/articles/200704/daycare-raising-baby

Mason, C. (2017). *A Philosophy of Education* . Jilliby: Living Book Press.

McLeod, S. (2016, February 5). *Albert Bandura's Social Learning Theory*. Retrieved from Simply Psychology: https://www.simplypsychology.org/bandura.html

Medlin, D. R. (1994). Predictors of Achievement in Home-Educated Children: Aptitude, Self-Concept, and Pedagogical Practices. *The Homeschool Researcher*, 1-7.

Medlin, R. G. (2007). Homeschooled Children's Social Skills. *Home School Researcher*, 1-8.

Mesrobian, C. (2021, July 26). *What Is Waldorf Education? Exploring This Approach to Early Childhood Education.* Retrieved from Rasmussen.edu: https://www.rasmussen.edu/degrees/education/blog/what-is-waldorf-education/

Min Jeong Kang, M. H. (2009). The Wick in the Candle of Learning: Epistemic Curiosity Activates Reward Circuitry and Enhances Memory. *Association for Psychological Science*, 963-973.

Montessori Northwest. (n.d.). *What is Montessori Education?* Retrieved from Montessori Northwest: https://montessori-nw.org/about-montessori-education

PhD, P. D. (2009). *Smart but Scattered: The Revolutionary "Executive Skills" Approach to Helping Kids Reach Their Potential.* New York: Guilford Press.

Prachi E. Shah, H. M. (2018). Early childhood curiosity and kindergarten reading and math academic achievement. *Pediatric Research*, 380-386. Retrieved from https://www.nature.com/articles/s41390-018-0039-3

Ray, B. (2015). African American Homeschool Parents'
Motivations for Homeschooling and Their Black
Children's Academic Achievement. *Journal of School
Choice*, 9:71-96.

Schoolsmith. (2019, Feb 5). *A short history of education in
England*. Retrieved from Schoolsmith:
https://www.schoolsmith.co.uk/history-of-
education/

Seifert, M. (n.d.). *Grade 1*. Retrieved from Waldorf Teacher
Resources:
https://www.waldorfteacherresources.com/index.ph
p?topid=1&grade=1

Shields, J. S. (2016). Dyslexia: 10 Strategies. *TEACH Journal of
Christian Education*, 13-22.

Shrier, C. (2014, June 27). *Young Children Learn by Copying
You!* Retrieved from Michigan State University
Extension:
https://www.canr.msu.edu/news/young_children_le
arn_by_copying_you

Sophie von Stumm, B. H.-P. (2011). The Hungry Mind:
Intellectual Curiosity Is the Third Pillar of Academic
Performance. *Sage Journals*, 574-588.

The Relationship Between Incarceration and Low Literacy.
(n.d.). Retrieved from Literacy Mid-South:

https://www.literacymidsouth.org/news/the-
relationship-between-incarceration-and-low-literacy

ThinkImpact.com. (2022). *Homeschooling Statistics.*
Retrieved from www.thinkimpact.com:
https://www.thinkimpact.com/homeschooling-
statistics

University of Edinburgh. (2021, September). *CALL Scotland.*
Retrieved from www.callscotland.org.uk:
https://www.callscotland.org.uk/common-
assets/cm-files/posters/ipad-apps-for-complex-
communication-support-needs.pdf

Weller, C. (2015, September 3). *There's a New Path to
Harvard and it's not in a Classroom.* Retrieved from
Business Insider:
https://www.businessinsider.com/homeschooling-
is-the-new-path-to-harvard-2015-9

Why Colleges are Recruiting Homeschoolers. (2013,
September 5). Retrieved from Alpha Omega
Publications: https://www.aop.com/blog/why-
colleges-are-recruiting-homeschoolers

Wile, D. J. (2010, December 6). *Homeschool Graduates are
Amazingly Well-Rounded.* Retrieved from Proslogion:
https://blog.drwile.com/homeschool-graduates-are-
amazingly-well-rounded/

Zinsser, D. N. (2022). *The Confident Mind.* New York: Custom House.

About the Author

Kristy Crandall is a passionate advocate for homeschooling, empowering parents to take charge of their children's education. She's the COO and cofounder of The Homeschool Safari- an online support website for parents.

www.ingramcontent.com/pod-product-compliance
Lightning Source LLC
Chambersburg PA
CBHW041158150726
48006CB00016B/2027